JN450055

Basic course for Maritime English

HyunWook Doo · DaeWon Kim · SeongWan Kim
SangSeop Lim · HyeonMin Jeon · JungHwan Choi

Publishing company
GS INTERVISION

Basic Course for Maritime English

Copyright © Agust. 2022

HyunWook Doo, DaeWon Kim, SeongWan Kim, SangSeop Lim, HyeonMin Jeon, JungHwan Choi

Published by GSINTERVISION
Edited by SunKyung Lee

ISBN 979-11-5576-293-6 (93530)

Publishing company
GS INTERVISION

gsinter7@gmail.com
http://gsintervision.co.kr
tel : +82-2-976-7898 fax : +82-2-6468-7898
69, Jeungsan-ro 15-gil, Eunpyeong-gu, Seoul, Republic of Korea, 2nd floor

PREFACE

The shipping industry is a kind of industry that emphasizes internationality. In modern society, where movement between countries has become less restricted, and the importance of macroeconomic activities has been emphasized, supplies transported by ships are the driving force of the shipping industry. Since ancient times, seafarers have been on board ships, and even now, the duties of a seafarer are focused on the operation of ships. However, according to the change of the times, the profession of seafarers along with the shipping industry has taken on an international character, and the history of the STCW Convention, which standardized the seafarers' minimum competence, is also heading for half a century.

The STCW Convention, such an international standard for seafarers' training and certification, stipulates maritime English as a minimum competence commonly required for ship officers (navigator and engineer). In addition, recognized education institutes that train cadets provide maritime English courses. In particular, the faculty in charge of maritime English wrote a textbook based on the STCW Convention and IMO's model course by themselves and used it for lectures, so there were a lot of difficulties in investing much time and effort. Furthermore, the quality of the textbook also affected the satisfaction of students and the effectiveness of lectures.

Moreover, it is true that the maritime English textbook reflects the characteristics of the job of a ship officer and deals with various and specialized contents, which is helpful in practice, but it is also true that there were difficulties among students who were new to ships do not understand the terminology. As such, faculty members from Korea Institute of Maritime and Fisheries Technology, Korea Maritime & Ocean University, and Dalian Maritime University in China, who were concerned about various problems in the classroom, came together to prepare the Basic course for Maritime English for future ship officers taking their first steps in the shipping industry.

This book is a maritime English textbook based on the knowledge and competence that should be commonly required to a ship officer beyond the frame of textbooks for each navigator and engineer classified according to the duty of the ship officer. In some ways, the purpose is to maximize the effect of an advanced maritime English course following after basic maritime English course. Above all, the purpose of teaching foreign languages is to improve practical communication skills, so the authors focused on helping students use maritime English a lot in the classroom with various missions. We wish that this book would help students participate in the advanced maritime English classes and work on ships.

Through many meetings and discussions, we tried to improve the level of completion, and I think that there will be many shortcomings from the reader's point of view. We kindly ask for your sincere comments and support to be developed gradually as the years go by.

We are deeply grateful to GS Intervision for publishing this book despite the difficult situation caused by COVID-19 since 2020 and finally end with praying for the well-being and von voyage of seafarers at sea.

August. 2022

All the authors

머리글

해운산업은 국제성이 강조되는 산업이다. 국가 간의 이동이 자유로워지고 거시경제활동의 중요성이 강조되는 현대 사회에서 선박을 통한 물류 이송은 해운산업의 원동력이다. 예부터 선박에는 선원이 있었으며 지금도 여전히 선원의 직무는 선박 운항에 중점을 두고 있다. 다만 시대의 변화에 따라 해운산업과 함께 선원직도 국제성을 띠게 되었으며 선원의 해기능력을 표준화한 STCW협약의 역사도 반세기를 향하고 있다. 선원 교육 및 훈련의 국제표준인 STCW협약은 해기사에게 공통으로 요구되는 필수 해기능력으로서 해사영어(Maritime English)를 규정하고 있으며 해기사를 배출하는 해양계 고등학교와 대학교 그리고 한국해양수산연수원에서는 해사영어를 가르치고 있다. 특히, 해사영어를 담당하는 교수가 STCW협약 그리고 IMO의 모델코스를 근거로 교재를 집필하여 강의에 활용하다 보니 많은 시간과 노력을 투자해야 하는 애로사항이 있었으며 교육기관마다 다른 교재를 사용하다 보니 교재의 질이 강의의 만족도와 효과에 영향을 끼치기도 했다. 더욱이 시중의 교재가 해기사 직무의 특성을 반영하여 다양하고 전문적인 내용을 다루고 있어 실무에 도움이 되지만, 선박을 처음 접하는 학생에게는 용어부터 어렵다는 학생들의 불만이 아닌 볼멘소리가 있었던 것도 사실이다. 이처럼 강의실의 여러 소소한 문제를 고민한 한국해양수산연수원, 한국해양대학교 그리고 중국 대련해사대학교의 교수진이 뜻을 모아 이제 해운산업에 첫발을 내딛는 미래의 해기사를 위한 기초 해사영어 교재를 마련하게 되었다.

본서는 선박의 직무의 성격에 따라 분류된 항해사와 기관사에게 특화된 교재의 틀을 벗어나 해기사라고 한다면 공통으로 알고 있어야 할 해기능력과 지식을 기반으로 한 해사영어 교재다. 어떻게 보면 전문교육을 받기 이전에 기초교육을 시행함으로써 후에 실시되는 교육의 효과를 극대화하기 위한 목적을 가지고 있다. 무엇보다도 외국어의 교육목적은 실무적인 소통 능력을 향상시키는 데 있기에 다양한 mission을 담아 학생들이 해사영어를 강의실에서 많이 사용하도록 하는 데 중점을 두었다. 이러한 저자의 의도가 다소나마 학생들에게 상급과정 해사영어의 수업 참여와 선박에서 근무하는 데 도움이 됐으면 하는 마음이다.

많은 회의와 토론을 거치면서 참여 교수진들이 완성도를 높이기 위해서 노력하였지만 독자 입장에서 부족하고 미흡한 부분도 많이 보이리라 생각된다. 해를 거듭할수록 더욱 발전되는 모습으로 변모할 수 있도록 독자 여러분의 진심 어린 질책과 성원을 부탁한다.

2020년부터 전 세계적으로 유행한 COVID-19로 인한 어려운 여건 속에서도 출판을 맡아주신 GS인터비전에 깊이 감사드리며 지금도 해양에 있는 우리 선원의 안녕과 안전 항해를 기원하며 글을 맺는다.

2022년 8월

저자 일동

Contents

1

Introduction

1.1 Purpose

With the development of science and technology, ships and various machinery and devices are also being advanced and automated. Still, the reality is that the safe operation of vessels depends entirely on the seafarers' capabilities.

Multinational crew onboard ships are global trend. It is common that they are using English on board to carry out proper working and have a daily life. Although English has been recognised as a working language in international business, there is no mandatory requirement for English to be used on board in international rules and regulations. However, the English proficiency of deck officers and engineers is the minimum requirement in the shipping industry under the International Convention on Standards of Training, Certification and Watchkeeping for Seafarers (STCW), 1978. It provides that they shall have the English communication skill to perform their duties successfully.

Since seafarers onboard consist of multi-nationalities and frequently visit foreign countries, they shall be able to use general English for daily communication. Also ultimately, STCW Convention requires seafarers to be familiar with marine terminology related to on board duties or technical terms used only in the shipping industry as English for a special purpose. This book is developed to provide ship's officer, engineer and cadets with basic maritime English based on IMO model training courses of STCW Convention.It is written under consideration of the level of beginners who do not have working experience on board and have not yet acquired general knowledge about the ship's structure, equipment, and operation. In the case of cadets or trainees, they are not familiar with various marine terminology or technical terms. Furthermore, the main reason why they are not interested in Maritime English classes is concerned with the lack of general maritime knowledge.

Authors had have a common thought that the use of advanced Maritime English textbooks is inconvenienced to students or merchant marine cadets due to the high level of difficulty. Authors have decided to develop a basic courses for Maritime English to encourage high-level education institutions to use the text book for students or merchant marine cadets as practical as possible. This book will give beginners who wish to work at shipping industry a chance to increase their knowledge and understand Maritime English.

1.2 Composition and Utilization

1.2.1 Composition

This book consists of 11 Chapters. Chapters 2 to 10 are mainly focused on ships rather than professional and theoretical content since in the case of cadets who do not have experience onboard, they lack knowledge about the onboard oorganisation ship type, and various facilities (navigation equipment / engine machinery / deck machinery, etc.) It is structured so that the readers can become familiar with the terms and expressions, and pictures and illustrations are attached to help thier understanding. In particular, even though roles and duties of seafarers are relatively clarified, general and broad maritime knowledge about navigation or marine engineering is required to ensure the safety of navigation via cooperative relationship.

Table 1.1 Content

No.	Title	Main contents
1	Introduction	Brief introduction of the book and utilization
2	Seafarers and Duty	Onboard environment, seafarer organization, seafarer's duty, etc.
3	Ship and Port	The various types of ship and their function
4	General Arrangement	Ship structure and machinery arrangement
5	Engine System	Main engine and auxiliary machineries
6	Cargo	Cargo operation and ballasting

7	Maneuvering	Ship maneuvering and emergency response
8	Navigation & Engine Watch	Navigation equipment, bridge and engine room watchkeeping
9	Fire and Life Saving Equipment	Fire - fighting appliances, life-saving appliances and onboard drill
10	Relevant International Organization	International organizations and the concerned parties
11	Stakeholders in Shipping Industry	Private and public sector in shipping industry
·	Appendix	Articles and technical papers link
·	Maritime Words	Technical words

1.2.2 Utilization

This book was written in English to enable students and professors to communicate in English during class. Since the class consists of students with different English levels, it is recommended to form a group (4 to 6 cadets) considering the English level so that the facilitator control and instruct cadets easily. We intended to include many exercises and assignments in the textbook so that cadets can actively participate in class and use English as much as possible. It is recommended that exercises and assignments in this book should be shared in the way of a group or a intervention, so as to provide students with a presentation opportunity as much as possible. Students should try to use English during class as directed by their facilitators. Beyond the existing reading and listening - focused English classes, various English classes are conducted using this textbook so that reading, listening, speaking, and writing skills can be developed evenly. The use of English in this textbook helps students develop the four competencies through the exercise below.

(1) Utilization of English textbooks – Reading, writing, speaking & listening

Develop reading & writing skills through the text content and writing exercises of textbooks composed of various topics. In addition, you can read the sentences yourself and verify your pronunciation and vocabulary skills through the recorded results.

(2) English lessons by instructors – Listening

After reviewing the students' level, a specific part of the class is conducted in English to develop the students' listening skills.

(3) Understanding maritime words – Words

Students can understand maritime technology by learning various specific maritime words for each subject with pictures.

(4) Summary – Writing

Exercise Chapter.2

1. Write down key words in this chapter.

2. Summarize the content in this chapter.

Fig. 1.1 Work sheet

By summarizing the main text of each chapter and arranging important words, writing ability can be cultivated.

(5) Speed quiz (pictures and words) – Speaking & listening

You can use various English expressions and explain maritime words based on the speed quiz game.

✓ **Speed Quiz** – Explain the function of machinery and Answer the word

✓ **Speed Quiz** – Explain the meaning of the word and Answer the word

Main engine	Propulsion	Generator engine	Boiler	Lubricating oil
Refrigeration system	Accommodation	Cargo handling	Fuel oil	Auxiliary machineries
Tank	Heater	Purifier	Filter	Valve
Pipeline	Temperature	Pressure	Scavenge air	Combustion
Control system	Alarm	Monitoring system	Starting air supply system	Shaft
Bed plate	Frame box	Cylinder frame	Governor	Injection timing
Bridge	Engine control room	Engine speed	Turbocharger	Piston crown
Cylinder liner	Crank shaft	Propeller	Intermediate shaft	Crankshaft
Bearing	Incinerator	Hydraulic power	Navigation	Equipment
Black out	Emergency	Merchant ships	Cooling system	Main switch board
Starter panel	Synchronizing panel	Local group starter panel	Viscosity	Polar

Fig. 1.2 Speed quiz

(6) Role playing – Reading, listening, speaking & writing

Infer the maritime word for a given situation, and write a sentence suitable for the situation. A script suitable for each topic and situation is created and presented to the other students through team building.

Instructors and students will have a variety of time to utilise English by evaluating the role-play of the presenters from an objective point of view. It is also a good time for students to raise their confidence and competency in English.

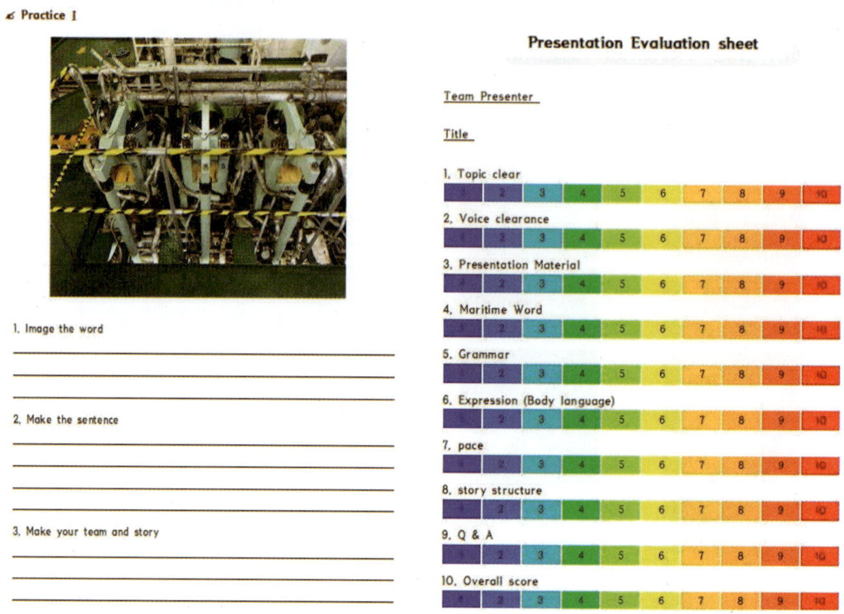
Practice I

1. Image the word

2. Make the sentence

3. Make your team and story

Presentation Evaluation sheet

Team Presenter

Title

1. Topic clear
2. Voice clearance
3. Presentation Material
4. Maritime Word
5. Grammar
6. Expression (Body language)
7. pace
8. story structure
9. Q & A
10. Overall score

Fig. 1.3 Role play and evaluation sheet

(7) Video material – Listening & writing

It is intended to enhance understanding of key situations and terms related to each chapter topic through video.

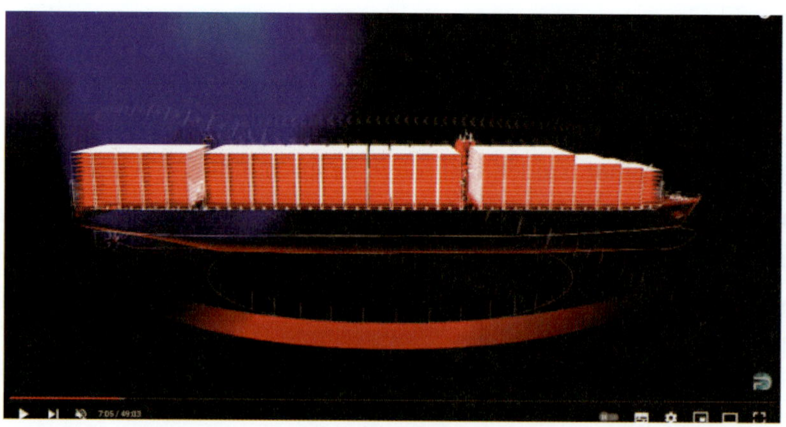

Fig. 1.4 Video

(8) Utilization of appendix – Reading & writing

Through articles related to the latest regulations and technologies, it is possible to comprehend significant maritime technical terms and summarise the contents.

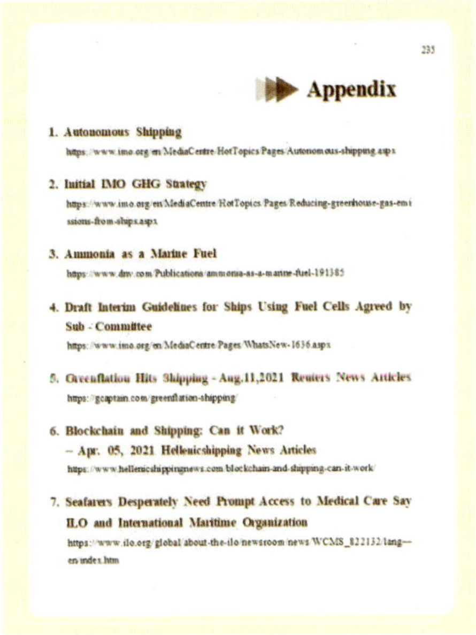

235

Appendix

1. **Autonomous Shipping**
   https://www.imo.org/en/MediaCentre/HotTopics/Pages/Autonomous-shipping.aspx
2. **Initial IMO GHG Strategy**
   https://www.imo.org/en/MediaCentre/HotTopics/Pages/Reducing-greenhouse-gas-emissions-from-ships.aspx
3. **Ammonia as a Marine Fuel**
   https://www.dnv.com/Publications/ammonia-as-a-marine-fuel-191385
4. **Draft Interim Guidelines for Ships Using Fuel Cells Agreed by Sub - Committee**
   https://www.imo.org/en/MediaCentre/Pages/WhatsNew-1636.aspx
5. **Greenflation Hits Shipping - Aug.11,2021 Reuters News Articles**
   https://gcaptain.com/greenflation-shipping/
6. **Blockchain and Shipping: Can it Work?**
   – Apr. 05, 2021 Hellenicshipping News Articles
   https://www.hellenicshippingnews.com/blockchain-and-shipping-can-it-work/
7. **Seafarers Desperately Need Prompt Access to Medical Care Say ILO and International Maritime Organization**
   https://www.ilo.org/global/about-the-ilo/newsroom/news/WCMS_822132/lang--en/index.htm

Fig. 1.5 Technical paper links

(9) Voice recording – Speaking & listening

By recording the text in your voice and listening to it, you can correct pronunciation, difficult - to - read words, unknown words, keywords, and interrupted reading of sentences.

2

Seafarers and Duty

2.1 Environment
2.2 Organization
2.3 Duty
2.4 Life at Sea

2.1 Environment

The main task of seafarers onboard is to safely transport cargo loaded on the ship to the port. To this end, they do their best to ensure that the ship operates safely by performing on-call duties for a certain period according to the given time. The ship itself can be seen as another society. There is a living area for seafarers to rest and an area for seafarers to work. As we usually live comfortably in our own homes, there are various cultural facilities such as restaurants, laundry rooms, restrooms, gymnasiums, saunas, and baths for seafarers onboard the ships. Life onboard has to fight the weather and waves from the outside, and living on an iron plate has various difficulties due to noises and vibrations generated from the equipment. However, just like a doctor treats human life, seafarers perform their duties with significant responsibility to ensure that ships operate safely. In this process, they perform their duties with great satisfaction.

The dictionary meanings of seafarers that we generally use are as follows.

"Someone who works or travels on a boat or ship on the sea"

It is recommended that exercises and assignments in this book should be shared in the way of a group or a intervention, so as to provide students with a presentation opportunity as much as possible. In addition, we will learn about the life of seafarers on board. Many other words refer to seafarer, such as sailor, mariner, hand, and seamen. The words for seafarers mean various roles depending on the type of ship and the duties of the seafarers.

2.2 Organization

What are a seafarer and officer?

A seafarer is someone who works or travels on a boat or a ship at sea. Moreover, an officer (including an engineer officer) refers to a person who acquires professional knowledge on ship operation, ship engine operation, and ship communication and has passed the national qualification test and obtained a prescribed license.

Captain and officer

The captain is in charge of the ship and has the authority to take responsibility and command the ship's safety and human life by various regulations. The captain confirms the voyage destination, climate, distance, Etc., before departure and instructs the ship's speed and route using charts, compass, radar, automatic ship identification system (AIS), and other navigation devices when sailing.

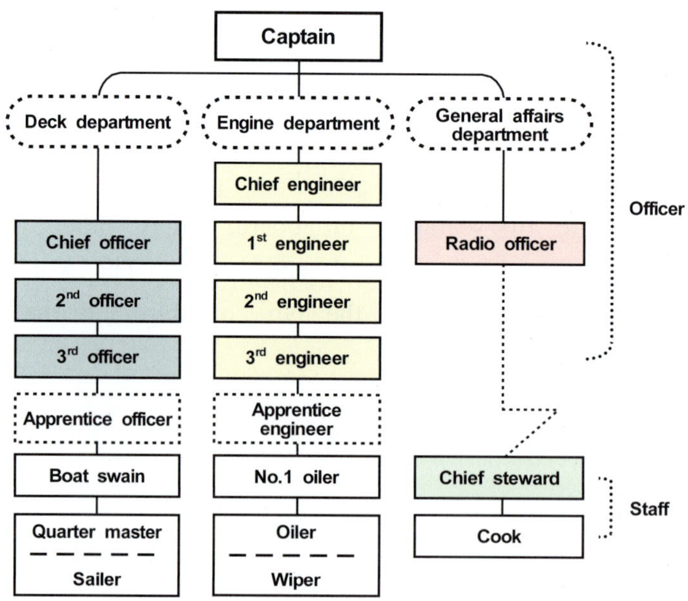

Fig. 2.1 Ship organization chart

The first officer assists the captain and plans and supervises establishing rules within the ship, various education, and training for junior officers and crew members, safety management, and cargo loading. The second officer manages navigational instruments on board, charts, and navigation-related books. The third officer manages emergency medical care, and fire extinguishing facilities for a ship.

Fig. 2.2 Navigation bridge in ship

Engineer officer

The chief engineer is the head of the engine department, assists the captain, and controls the engine department. The first engineer assists the head of the engine department, is in charge of the main engine and related equipment and performs the personnel management of the system. The second and third engineers manage fuel oil and lubricating oil and are in charge of various auxiliary engines, including generators and boilers, respectively. Engineers take turns performing watch duties, and these days, they are working at an unmanned vessel (UMA) so that the ship's engine equipment can be operated safely 24 hours a day.

Fig. 2.3 Engine room in ship

In addition to officers, some people help the officers and operate the ship, such as deck crew members, engine crew members, and chief steward members.

2.3 Duty

2.3.1 Captain (master)

- As a shipowner's representative, overseeing all internal affairs for the safety and environmental protection of ships, seafarers, and cargo
- Safe operation of ships and protection and management of human and property
- Seafarer's command and supervision, the establishment of ship discipline, and maintenance of order.
- Efforts to increase the economic operation of ships and business profits
- Storage and management of mandatory and essential documents
- Work-related shifting of boarding and disembarking ships of seafarers

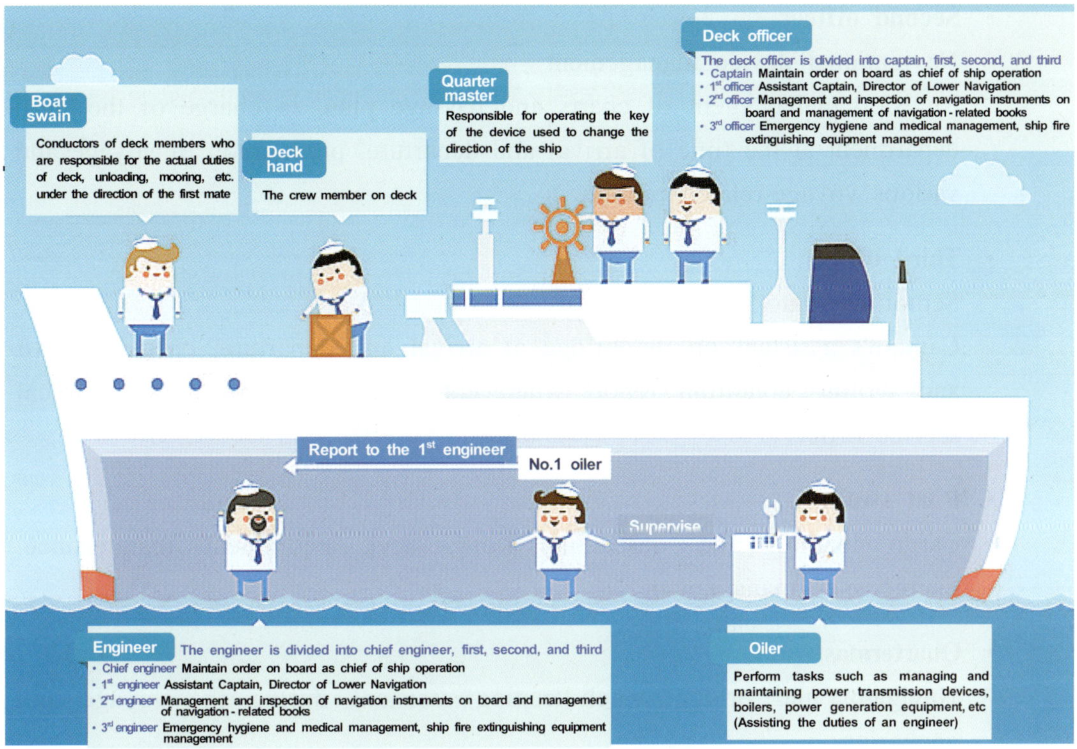

Fig. 2.4 Seafarer's role

2.3.2 Deck department

The main tasks are assigned to the deck include safe operation of ships, navigation and berthing watch, cargo and unloading-related businesses, maintenance of safety facilities and related equipment onboard medical care, hygiene-related tasks, etc.

- **Chief officer**

  Assistant to the captain and acting in case of absence of the captain
  Supervising the work of the deck department, confirming and supervising the establishment of the cargo loading and unloading work plan, directing the work of the deck members, in charge of the bow department at the time of entry and departure, and responsible for the discipline relationship on the ship

- **Second officer**
  Navigational device management
  Revision management of charts and passage plan, in charge of the stern department at the time of arrival and departure, preparation of voyage and various voyage-related reports

- **Third officer**
  Senior navigator's assistant
  Captain's assistant on the bridge at arrival and departure, checking draft and writing condition report when entering and leaving port, medical service officer

- **Boat swain**
  Cargo loading and unloading work, deck equipment maintenance, maintenance management

- **Quartermaster**
  Navigator and bridge watch-keeping assistant during the voyage and anchoring

- **Sailor**
  Onboard work and cargo handling under the command of the boatswain.

When a ship is entered into a port, the first and second officers perform duties according to the captain's order at the front and stern positions in a ship. The third officer transmits the ship's position and sends the captain's commands to the bow, stern position, and engine control room.

2.3.3 Engine department

The main tasks are related to operation and maintenance of the main engine and auxiliary machinery, including cargo machinery. Bunkering for fuel oil and lubricating oils. Data recording and engine watch.

- **Chief engineer**
  Head of the engine department
  The overall operation and maintenance of the engine system of the ship
  Responsibility for fuel oil management, plan establishment, and implementation of energy-saving measures
  Pollution prevention manager, ship's machinery inspection preparation and inspection management, engine department supplies management

- **First engineer**
  An engineer in charge of the overall engine room including engine maintenance work

- **Second engineer**
  An engineer in charge of the generator and fuel oil / waste oil management

- **Third engineer**
  An engineer of auxiliary equipment such as a boiler, a fresh water generator, air conditioning system, etc

- **No.1 oiler**
  Support engineers for maintenance, repair work of engine department, and deck welding work. Supervising the rating's work in the engine department

- **Oiler**
  Operation, maintenance, and repair of the engine machinery according to the instructions from engineers

- **Wiper**
  Maintain the cleanliness of the engine room, Support any work in the engine department

2.4 Life at Sea

Seafarers live in a separate bedroom in the accommodation. In some cases, a bedroom and a separate private office are given to the captain, chief engineer, chief officer and first engineer.

Fig. 2.5 Interior view of the seafarer's bedroom in the ship 1

Fig. 2.6 Interior view of the seafarer's bedroom in the ship 2

Fig. 2.7 Interior view of the seafarer's bedroom in the ship 3

A chief steward and a cook for seafarer's meals on ships since a few multinational seafarers are on board. Various types of food are served in consideration of the tastes and religions of each country by them.

Fig. 2.8 View of the ship's restaurant

Fig. 2.9 Seafarer's meals served on board

For the rest and leisure of seafarers, the ship's accommodation is equipped with a laundry room, a restroom, a library, a gymnasium, a table tennis room, a sauna, and a gymnasium bath, and a swimming pool, etc. By using these facilities, an environment is provided to seafarers to relieve the stress caused from sailing for a long time.

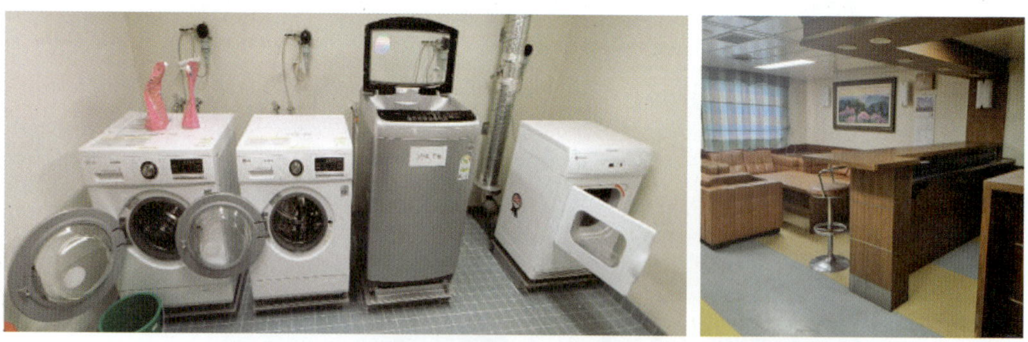

Fig. 2.10 Various resting facilities in the ship 1

Fig. 2.11 Various resting facilities in the ship 2

Fig. 2.12 Various resting facilities in the ship 3

Fig. 2.13 Various resting facilities in the ship 4

Fig. 2.14 Various resting facilities in the ship 5

Exercise

Chapter.2

1. Write down key words in this chapter.

2. Summarize the content in this chapter.

✓ **Speed Quiz** - Explain the picture below

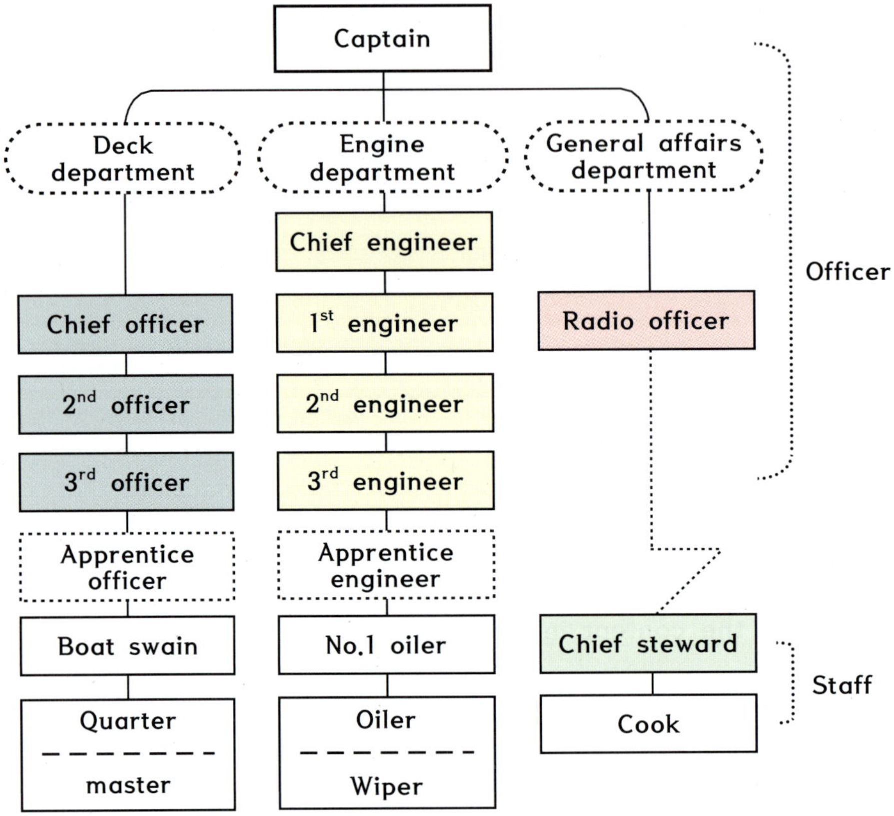

✓ **Speed Quiz** - Explain the role of a seafarer

Captain	No.1 oiler	Cook	Chief engineer	3rd engineer
Boat swain	Chief officer	1st engineer	2nd officer	Chief steward
2nd engineer	Quarter master	Wiper	Sailor	3rd officer

✍ Practice I

1. Image the word

2. Make the sentence

3. Make your team and story

4. Set the role

5. Presentation with video recording

6. Self-evaluation

7. Feedback

Presentation Evaluation sheet

Team Presenter ______

Title ______

1. Topic clear

1	2	3	4	5	6	7	8	9	10

2. Voice clearance

1	2	3	4	5	6	7	8	9	10

3. Presentation Material

1	2	3	4	5	6	7	8	9	10

4. Maritime Word

1	2	3	4	5	6	7	8	9	10

5. Grammar

1	2	3	4	5	6	7	8	9	10

6. Expression (Body language)

1	2	3	4	5	6	7	8	9	10

7. pace

1	2	3	4	5	6	7	8	9	10

8. story structure

1	2	3	4	5	6	7	8	9	10

9. Q & A

1	2	3	4	5	6	7	8	9	10

10. Overall score

1	2	3	4	5	6	7	8	9	10

✓ Feedback opinion

Date ______________

Evaluator ______________

3

Ship and Port

3.1 Dry Bulk Carrier

A dry bulk carrier or bulker is a ship that carries dry bulk such as grain and coal. Dry bulk accounts for a high share of more than 50% of the ship's cargo volume. The ship can transport cargo like wood or vehicles on deck. The bulk carrier has a cargo hatch cover to prevent the cargo from falling into the sea during transportation or distorting due to rain or seawater during navigation.

Fig. 3.1 Dry bulk carrier in port

Fig. 3.2 Dry bulk carrier – ore carrier

Fig. 3.3 Dry bulk carrier in port

There are many kinds of dry bulk cargoes, and the ships are operated irregularly, so they often enter small rather than large ports. In particular, in the case of small ports, there is no cargo unloading facility, so difficulties in shipping and unloading can be encountered. Therefore, loading cranes are installed in small or medium-size dry bulk carriers that can be ported to these ports.

3.2 Container Ship

A container ship is a ship to transport standardized containers. In general, the cargo characterized that there is no need to transport a large amount of cargo such as dry bulk, but demand is high and the various kinds of cargo such as food, electronic devices, etc. The box-shaped container carries cargoes at the same time. They are easy to load and unload from ports and are used for economical transportation that can be transported economically. It is easy to connect to other transportation methods.

The size of a container ship has become bigger than before, and it is mainly used for intercontinental transfer. A container ship's small and medium-size is being used for container transfer in regions and short distances. As the cargo has diversified, the container technology is also developing and used to transport such a small amount of hazardous materials through special containers and fruits through refrigerating containers to store food.

Fig. 3.4 Container ship at sea

Fig. 3.5 Container ship at sea

Fig. 3.6 Container ship in port

3.3 Tanker

The tanker is a ship that transports fluid products. The tanker was an oil tanker that transported crude oil, refinery products, or liquefied gas.

Since the tanker is a ship that transports energy cargo in large quantities, it is more likely to be exposed to danger than other cargo ships. The damage caused by marine accidents is more significant than other types of ships, so the ship safety requirements and crew education requirements have been strengthened.

In the United States Navy and Military Sealift Command, a tanker used to refuel other ships is called an oiler (or replenishment oiler if it can also supply dry stores). However, many other navies use the terms tanker and replenishment tanker. Tankers also carry commodities such as vegetable oils, molasses, and wine. Tankers were first developed in the late 19th century as iron and steel hulls, and pumping systems were developed. As of 2005, there were just over 4,000 tankers and supertankers 10,000 LT DWT or greater operating worldwide.

Fig. 3.7 Crude oil tanker at sea

The tanker segment can be divided into several sub-categories:

- Oil tankers
- Chemical Tankers

(1) Oil tankers

With the majority of oil and gas reserves located in a handful of countries and refineries and consumers located across the globe, oil tankers play a vital role in transporting crude oil and refined petroleum products to where they are needed. Typically, very Large Crude Carriers (VLCCs) carry crude oil from the oil extracted to the countries where the oil is refined into its products. These ships typically carry 350,000 tonnes of crude oil as a single cargo. Smaller tankers with a capacity of up to 35,000 tonnes, known as Product Tankers, distribute the petroleum products such as diesel, gas oil, lubricating oil, and petrol from the refineries to the ports servicing industrial consumers.

Product tankers are often designed also to carry chemical cargoes, which often requires special forms of construction and equipment such as the use of stainless steel in cargo tank construction, corrugated bulkheads, deep well pumps, and more complex piping systems. Oil tankers represent a crucial part of the energy supply chain and help ensure the security of supply.

(2) Chemical tankers

Chemical tankers carry a range of industrial chemicals and oil also clean petroleum products. Chemical cargoes carried are diverse and include caustic soda, sulphuric acid, and many other cargoes, all of which can present hazards from pollution and safety perspectives. Chemical tankers are designed, constructed, and operated based on the hazards to mitigate the risks. Chemical tankers, which have stainless steel or specially coated tanks, often also carry food products such as palm oil and vegetable oil.

Chemical tankers often carry small parcels of cargo, possibly carrying many different types of chemicals simultaneously. Different cargoes can be loaded, carried, and discharged separately without the risk of contamination. This is made possible by specially designing the cargo arrangements, e.g., many small cargo tanks and dedicated piping arrangements allowing systems onboard to be subdivided. Chemical cargoes can represent considerable risk and can be very dangerous, requiring high ship construction and operation standards. Chemical tankers make up an essential part of the industrial chain. For example, caustic soda is crucial in bauxite processing to make aluminum.

3.4 Gas Carriers

Gas carriers transport LPG or LNG, which are used in various applications, from heating, cooking, and transport, to electricity generation and other industrial uses. The distribution of these alternative energy sources to customers worldwide contributes to the energy supply chain and provides additional security to the global market.

Fig. 3.8 LNG carrier

3.5 Passenger Ship

A passenger ship is a ship that transports passengers. In order to be legally classified as a passenger ship, it must carry 13 or more passengers according to International Convention for the Safety of Life at Sea (SOLAS). Since the safety of human life at sea has been emphasized as a top priority, passenger ships' structure and facility standards are more strict than that of cargo ships. In modern society, cruise ships operated for leisure and tourism in addition to passenger ships for pure movement of passengers are becoming more common. A cruise ship is such a sea hotel, so it is not only a variety of entertainment facilities such as a passenger room, a restaurant, a theater, a sauna, a swimming pool, and a casino where passengers can enjoy leisure on board while sailing for a long period but medical center such as a hospital for people who need cares and treatments in case of emergency, a welfare facility such as childcare is also provided.

Fig. 3.9 Large cruise ship

3.6 Fishing Vessel

A vessel engaged in fishing is called a fishing vessel. It is the type of ship with the longest history with a human being. The fishing vessel has different fishing gears depending on the type of fishing, and many crew members are also working on board compared to the merchant ships. In addition, to prevent the depletion of fishery resources due to reckless fishing and preserve them for the next generation, the amount of catches and the tonnage of fishing vessels is limited.

Fig. 3.10 Fishing vessel

3.7 Other Ship

Ships are used for special purposes, such as hospital ships, fishing guidance ships, training ships, and customs ships. There are also coast guard ships and warships for maritime security purposes.

As leisure activities at sea become common, various types of leisure equipment are emerging, not traditional ships such as small leisure boats and yachts.

Fig. 3.11 Hospital ship

Fig. 3.12 Leisure boat

A heavy - lift ship is a vessel designed to move massive loads that regular ships cannot handle. They are of two types:

Semi - submersible ships take on water ballast to allow the load - usually another vessel - to be floated over the deck. The ballast is jettisoned, and the ship's deck and cargo are raised above the waterline.

Project cargo ships that use at least one heavy - lift crane for handling heavy cargo and sufficient ballast to assure stability and sea-keeping properties.

- **Semi - submersible ships**

Semi - submersible heavy - lift ships have a long low deck between a forward pilothouse and an Aft. machinery space. It is somewhat similar to a dry bulk carrier or some forms of an oil tanker's superficial appearance. Its ballast tanks can be flooded to lower the deck below the water's surface, allowing oil platforms, other vessels, or other floating cargo to be moved into position for loading (float - on / float - off). To balance the cargo, the various tanks can be pumped unevenly. The tanks are then pumped out, and the deck rises to shoulder the load.

- **Project cargo ships**

Project cargo ships are non - submersible ships that load large and heavy cargo items with one or more onboard cranes. Such vessels have between 13,000 and 19,000 deadweight tonnage (DWT) capacity. Cargo transport includes container cranes, bridge sections, and suction piles.

Fig. 3.13 A heavy lift ship

3.8 Port Facilities

Under the International Ship and Port Facility Security Code (ISPS Code) and regulations, security regulation are focused on the ship/port interface. This means that the definition of a port facility can be narrowly applied to wharves, berths, quays, and anchorages. These locations are where the loading and unloading of security - regulated ships occurs.

The term port facility means a specific location in a port where passengers or commodities are transferred between land and water carriers or between two water carriers, including wharves, piers, sheds, warehouses, yards, and docks. Ocean water terminals are classified as fixed-port facilities, unimproved port facilities, or bare beach port facilities. These facilities are further sub - classified as a general cargo terminal, container terminal, RO / RO terminal, and combination terminal. Usually, general cargo terminal operations apply to all ocean water terminals, while the rest of the three terminals apply to a fixed-port facility. The fixed port facility usually has state-of-the-art facilities and equipment. It is organized to support cargo discharge and port clearance operations.

Fig. 3.14 Container ship terminal

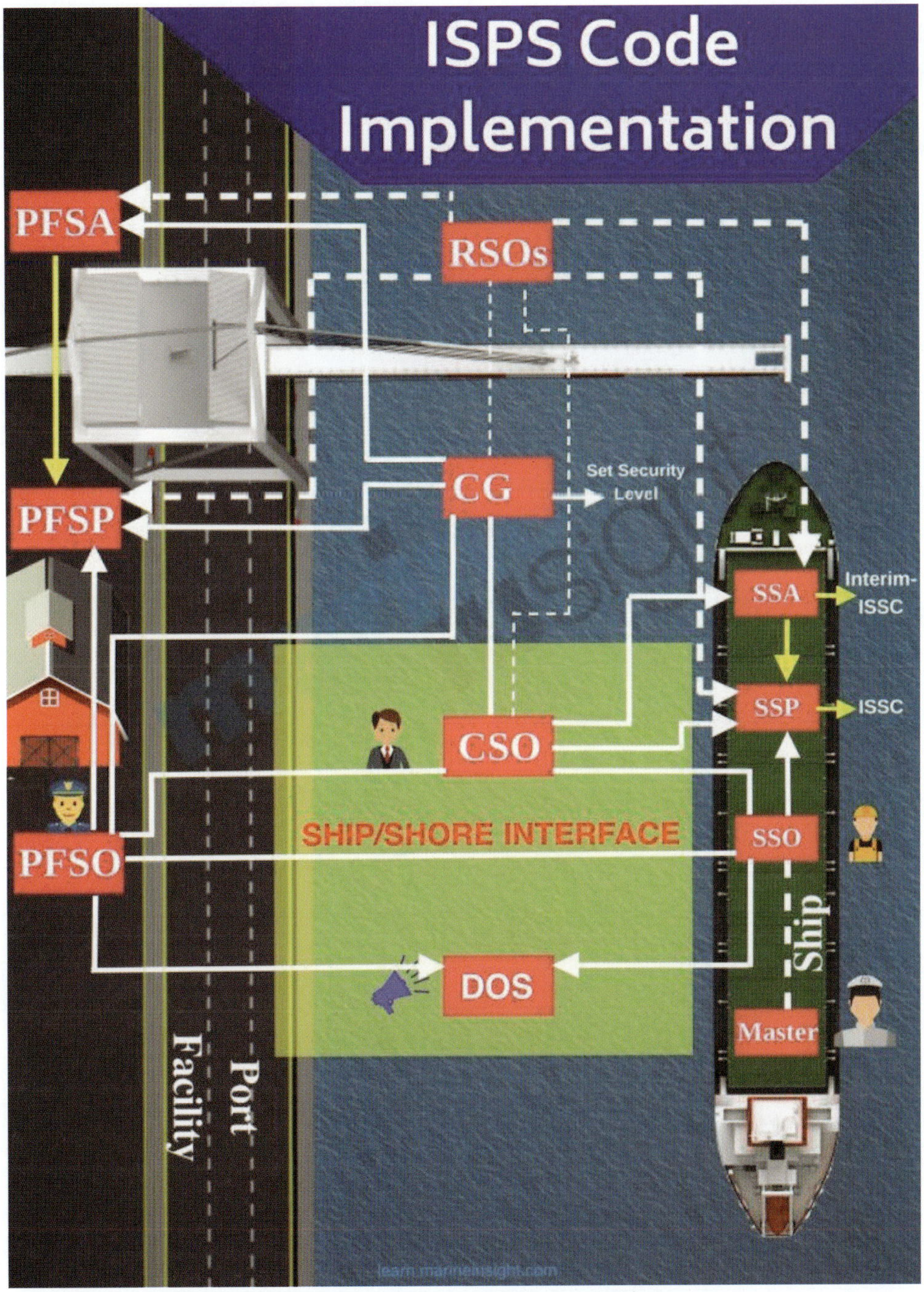

Fig. 3.15 ISPS Code implementation

Exercise

Chapter.3

1. Write down key words in this chapter.

2. Summarize the content in this chapter.

✓ **Speed Quiz** – Explain the meaning of the word and Answer the word

Bulk carrier	Container	Crude oil tanker	LPG carrier	LNG carrier
Chemical tanker	Fishing vessel	Passenger ship	Cruse ship	Heavy-lift ship
Semi - submersible ship	Container ship terminal			

✍ Practice

1. Image the word

2. Make the sentence

3. Make your team and story

4. Set the role

5. Presentation with video recording

6. Self-evaluation

7. Feedback

Presentation Evaluation sheet

Team Presenter ______

Title ______

1. Topic clear

1	2	3	4	5	6	7	8	9	10

2. Voice clearance

1	2	3	4	5	6	7	8	9	10

3. Presentation Material

1	2	3	4	5	6	7	8	9	10

4. Maritime Word

1	2	3	4	5	6	7	8	9	10

5. Grammar

1	2	3	4	5	6	7	8	9	10

6. Expression (Body language)

1	2	3	4	5	6	7	8	9	10

7. pace

1	2	3	4	5	6	7	8	9	10

8. story structure

1	2	3	4	5	6	7	8	9	10

9. Q & A

1	2	3	4	5	6	7	8	9	10

10. Overall score

1	2	3	4	5	6	7	8	9	10

✓ Feedback opinion

Date ____________________ Evaluator ____________________

4

General Arrangement

4.1 General Arrangement

A ship is an artificial structure composed of solid compartments that can withstand rough environments at sea, various installations and machines necessary for safe navigation and a living area where the crew can stay and rest. Although the installations and machines of the ship are different according to the ship's type, there is an engine room in which the propulsion machine called the main engine, generators for producing the electric power of the ship and other auxiliary machinery are installed in order to navigate safely. There is a bridge to watch and check the state of the sea and control the vessel. Windlasses and anchors allow the ships to stay in the port or keep the ship at the anchorage. Essentially, an accommodation facility where the crew can rest, have a meal and sleep is installed on the ship.

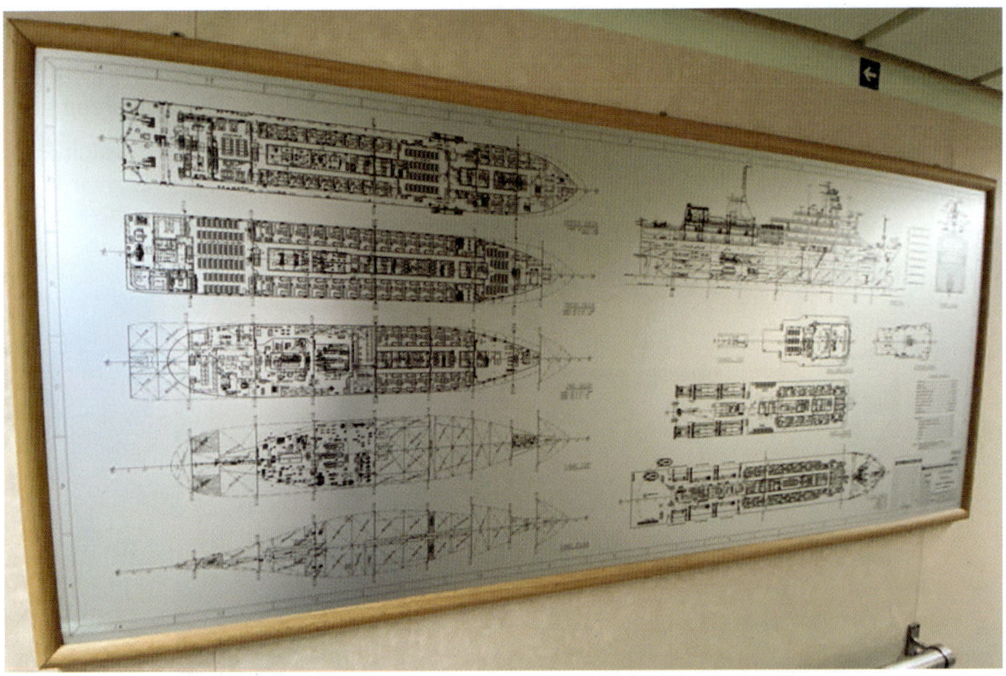

Fig. 4.1 General Arrangement

4.2 Bridge

A bridge is where the deck officers (navigators) generally work and where various navigational equipment is installed. As long as the vessel is at sea and in internal waters, the crew must be vigilant. As navigation using the Global Positioning System (GPS) became common, various electronic navigational equipment (Radar, Electric Chart Display and Information System) was installed on the bridge, and Ocean-navigation became safer and more convenient. In addition to navigational equipment, communication equipment that can contact other ships or land-based offices is installed on the bridge. In particular, the Global Maritime Distress and Safety System (GMDSS) is installed to promptly request the rescue when an emergency accident occurs due to a fire, a collision or when distress occurs due to a storm. Once the rescue signal is sent, INMARSAT (International Maritime Satellite Organization)'s artificial satellite quickly transmits it to the rescue center on the land. In addition, remote operation of the main engine related to the ship's steering is possible. The main engine can be operated on the bridge in a normal and an emergency by the watchkeeping officer.

Fig. 4.2 Bridge of training ship

4.3 Engine Room

The engine room is an area in which various machinery and other equipment are installed to enable ship's navigation. Since various machinery and equipment in the engine room are installed to operate the main engine, they are generally divided into the main and auxiliary machinery. The main engine is a machine that produces the propulsion power for the ship, and that is classified into an internal combustion engine and an external combustion engine according to the combustion method of fuel oil or gas. An internal combustion engine refers to a diesel engine in a ship, and an external combustion engine refers to a boiler that generates steam. However, combustion engines, which were the mainstream in the 20th, are gradually being converted to eco-friendly ship propulsion engines using LNG, biofuel oil, or electric power due to environmental pollution emitted from the combustion engines.

Fig. 4.3 Main engine in engine room

4.4 Accommodation

Accommodation is a facility where crew or people on board can rest after working. There are many facilities; the cabin is a private resting space and, a restaurant where the crew can eat and a galley where the food is cooked, a hospital room where the injured crew is quickly treated, an entertainment area where the crew can get together and take rests, and also fitness area where the crew exercise for their health. Since a ship is a large structure and various facilities and machines are installed, many vibrations and noise may occur. Therefore, the accommodation area should be designed to properly block and reduce external factors of ships and the sea environment that may impede the rest of the crew.

In general, a bridge is installed at the top of the accommodation area to ensure high visibility. There is also a muster area nearby where crews can quickly evacuate in an emergency. In addition, a control room to command the ship's emergency and an office for the crew is located.

4.5 Hull

A hull is the main and watertight body of a ship. It is plated from the outside and usually has a rectangular cross-section. When building a ship hull, the first thing being laid is a keel - the ship's backbone.

4.5.1 Layout and terminology

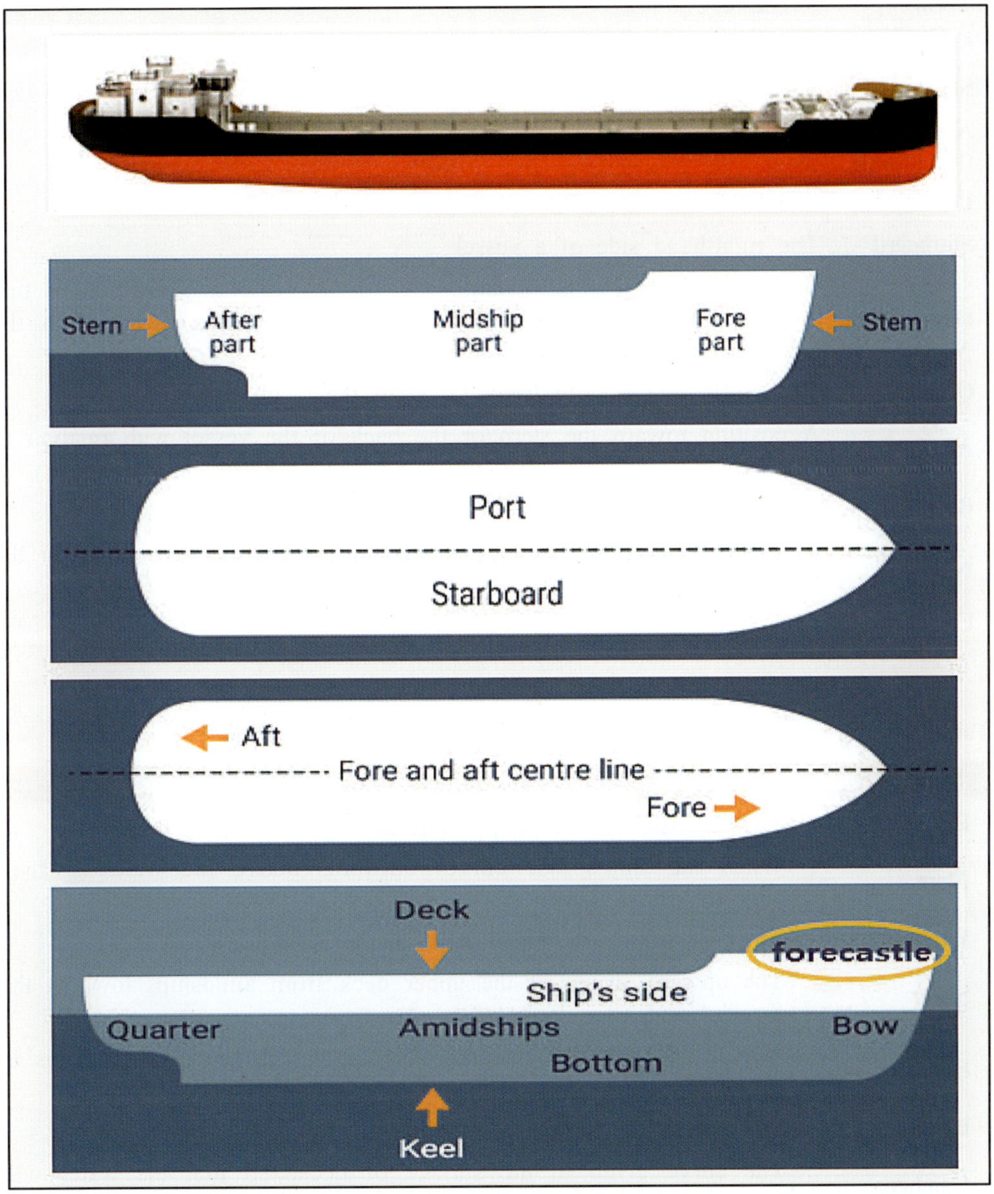

Source : https://maritimesa.org/nautical-science-grade-10/2020/12/10/layout-of-a-typical-ship-and-nautical-terms/

Fig. 4.4 Ship's hull

Table 4.1 Terms of ship's hull Ⅰ

Term	Meaning
Stern	After end of a vessel
Stem	Fore end of a vessel
Amidships (= midship)	The middle of the ship, either lengthwise or widthwise or both.
Port	The left-hand side of a vessel
Starboard	The right-hand side of a vessel
Deck	A principal horizontal component of a vessel's construction that consists of planking or plating at the surface and extending to the sides.
Quarter	A vessel's side usually from 45° abaft the beam to the stern.
Abaft	A position toward the stern or the back of the vessel with relation to another object on the vessel but not behind the vessel.
Bow	The forward part of a vessel.
Keel	A structural part that is the backbone of the ship; it runs along the centerline of the bottom.
Forecastle	The upper deck of forward section of a vessel

Table 4.2 Terms of ship's hull Ⅱ

Term	Meaning
Bulwark	The extension of the ship's side above the weather deck.
Flare	When the ship's side curves outwards above the waterline they are said to be flared.
Forefoot	The part of the stem that joins the keel
Sheer	The upward sweep of the upper deck from amidships towards the forward and after ends.
Bulbous bow	A type of bow in high-speed ships in which the entry expands in a bulbous shape so as to reduce the size of the bow wave.
Beam	The greatest width of the hull.
Camber	The curve given to the surface of decks so that the water will drain away to the sides.
Tumblehome	When the ship's side curves or slopes inward above the waterline they are said to tumble home.

Freeboard	The height of the highest continuous deck (upper deck) above the waterline at any point along the hull.
Draught	The depth of the keel below the waterline at any point along the hull.
Keel	A structural part that is the backbone of the ship; it runs along the centerline of the bottom.
Bilge keel	A longitudinal fin welded onto the sides of the ship's bottom to decrease the rolling of a ship. It is normally welded to the hull at the turn of the bilge.

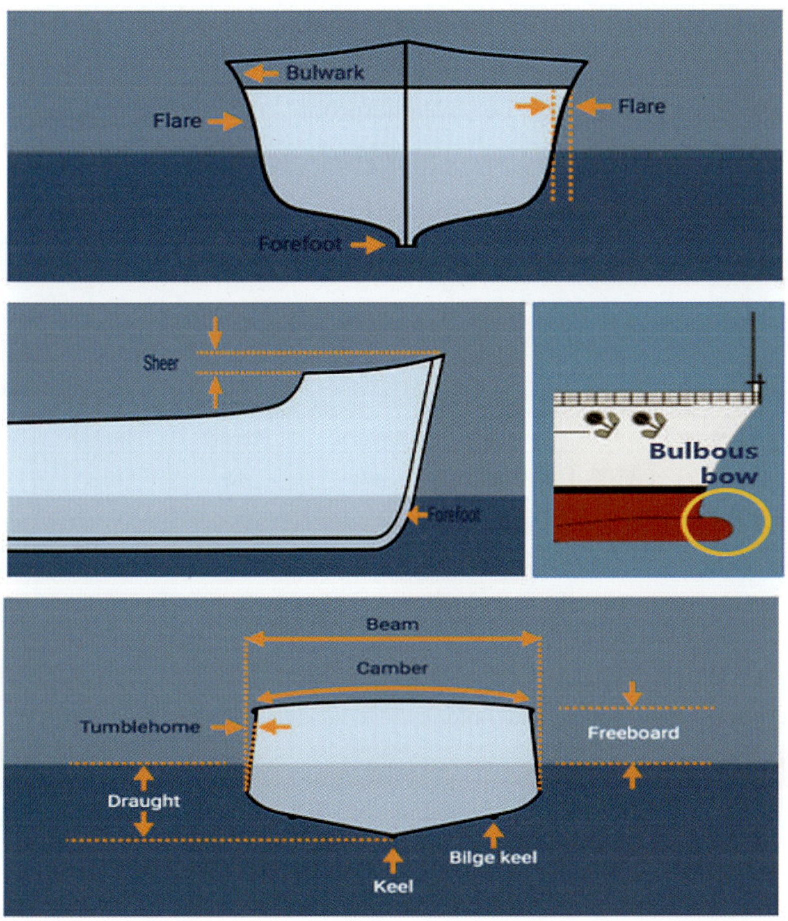

Source : https://maritimesa.org/nautical-science-grade-10/2020/12/10/layout-of-a-typical-ship-and-nautical-terms/

Fig. 4.5 Ship's hull Ⅱ

4.6 Cargo Hold

4.6.1 Layout and terminology

Decks are horizontal structures that divide the ship into levels. A deck is a permanent covering over a compartment or a ship's hull. They give the ship hull additional strength and rigidity and house internal spaces. A ship's hold or cargo hold is a space for carrying cargo in the ship's compartment. A hatch or hatch cover is a large steel structure fitted over a hatch opening to prevent water ingress into the cargo hold. It may also be the supporting structure for deck cargo. Various designs exist for particular applications. The hatch cover has to be weatherproof and must remain so when conditions change due to waves, temperature, and cargo.

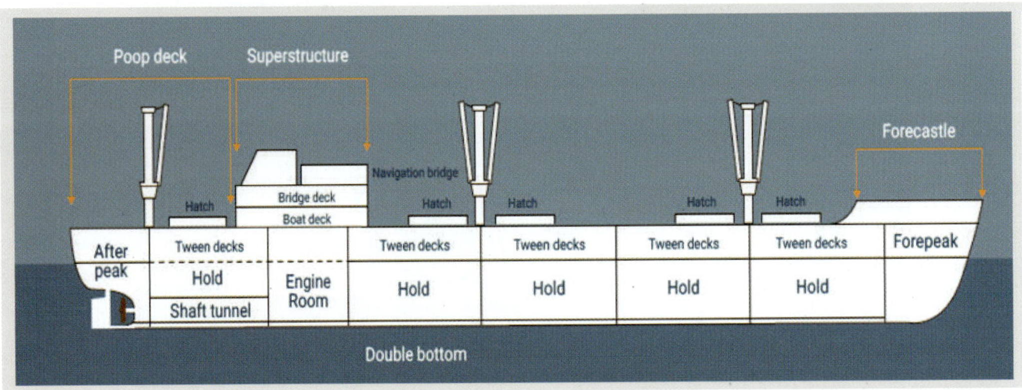

Fig. 4.6 Ship's deck and hold

Table 4.3 Terms of ship's deck and hold

Term	Meaning
Fore peak	The compartment forward of the farthest forward bulkhead, the space between the collision bulkhead and the stem.
After peak	The compartment at the stern after of the last watertight bulkhead.
Bulkhead	Transverse and longitudinal partitions separating portions of a vessel.

Forecastle	The Forward section of a vessel is reserved for the crew's quarters.
Hold	The below - deck cargo-holding spaces of a cargo vessel.
Tween deck	A deck between the upper deck and the hold.
Hatch	A watertight cover over an opening or hatchway that gives access to spaces below.
Superstructure	The structure built above the upper deck is called the superstructure. It consists of many decks housing, the accommodation or living quarters, offices, electronic equipment rooms, store rooms and the bridge.

A ballast voyage is a voyage with no cargo on board to get a ship in position for the next loading port or docking. On the voyage, the ship is said to be in ballast. The status of a laden ship refers to the state in which the cargo is loaded. Therefore, the voyage from a loading port to a destination port is called as 'laden voyage'.

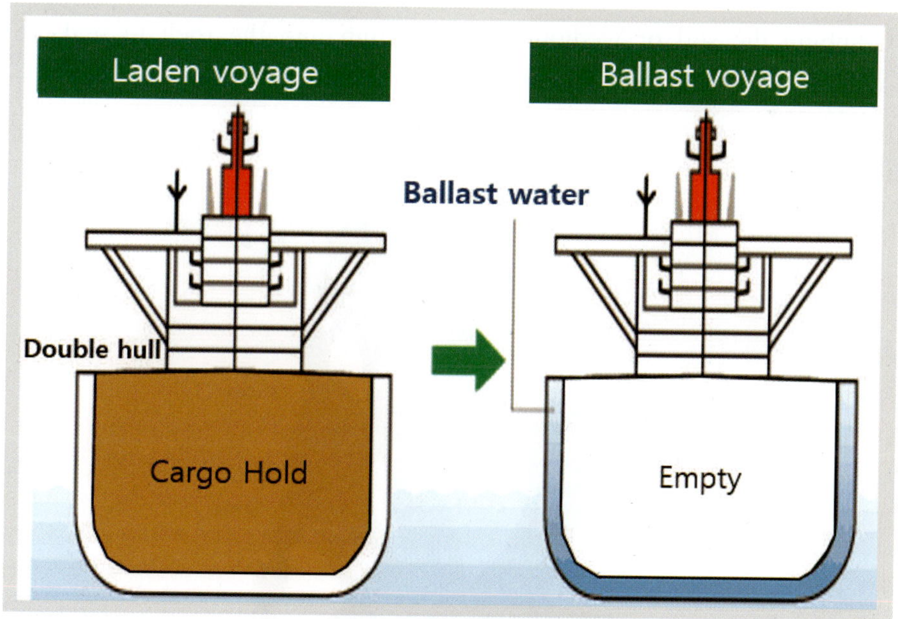

Fig. 4.7 Ballast and laden voyage

Table 4.4 Terms of ballast and laden voyage

Term	Meaning
Laden	Cargo loaded
Ballast	Water placed low in a vessel to increase stability.
Double hull	A double hull is a ship hull design and construction method where the bottom and sides of the ship have two complete layers of watertight hull surface

4.7 Anchoring and Mooring Equipment

Generally, anchors secure moorings and foundations in a fixed position on the seafloor. They are available in many types, relating to how they obtain the capability to maintain their position:

- The simple use of a large weight to resist uplift and sliding and the addition of features to enhance sliding resistance
- Grabbing the soil or wedging or cementing into the rock to make use of the seafloor's strength and weight

4.7.1 Anchor layout and terminology

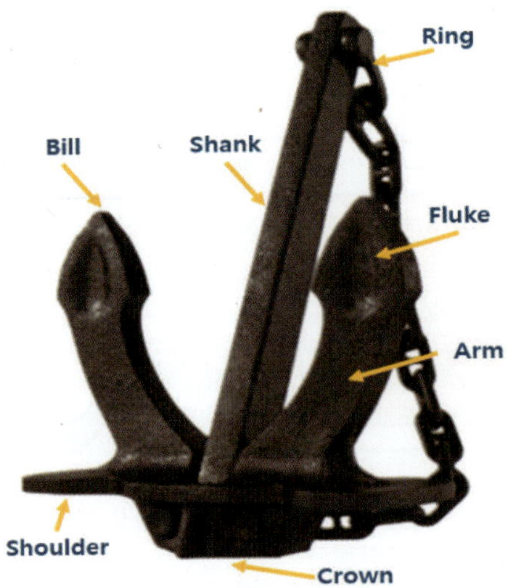

Fig. 4.8 Ship's anchor

4.7.2 Anchor system layout and terminology

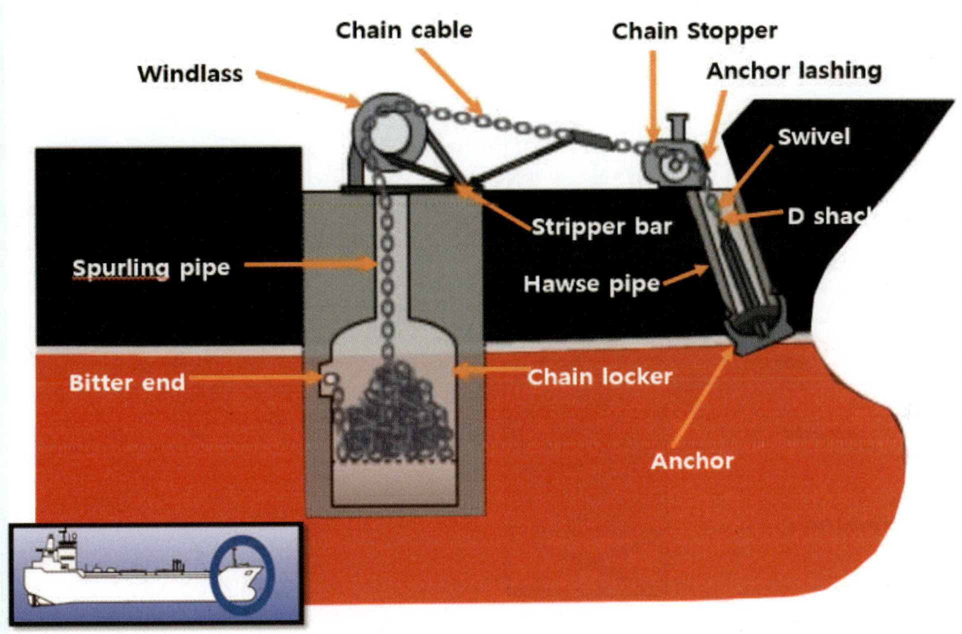

Source : http://shipsbusiness.com/anchoring-practice.html

Fig. 4.9 Anchoring system layout Ⅰ

4.7.3 Anchoring equipment

Anchoring equipment is designed for temporary mooring of a vessel within a harbour or sheltered area when the vessel is awaiting berth, etc. It is assumed that a ship will use only one bow anchor and chain cable at a time under normal circumstances.

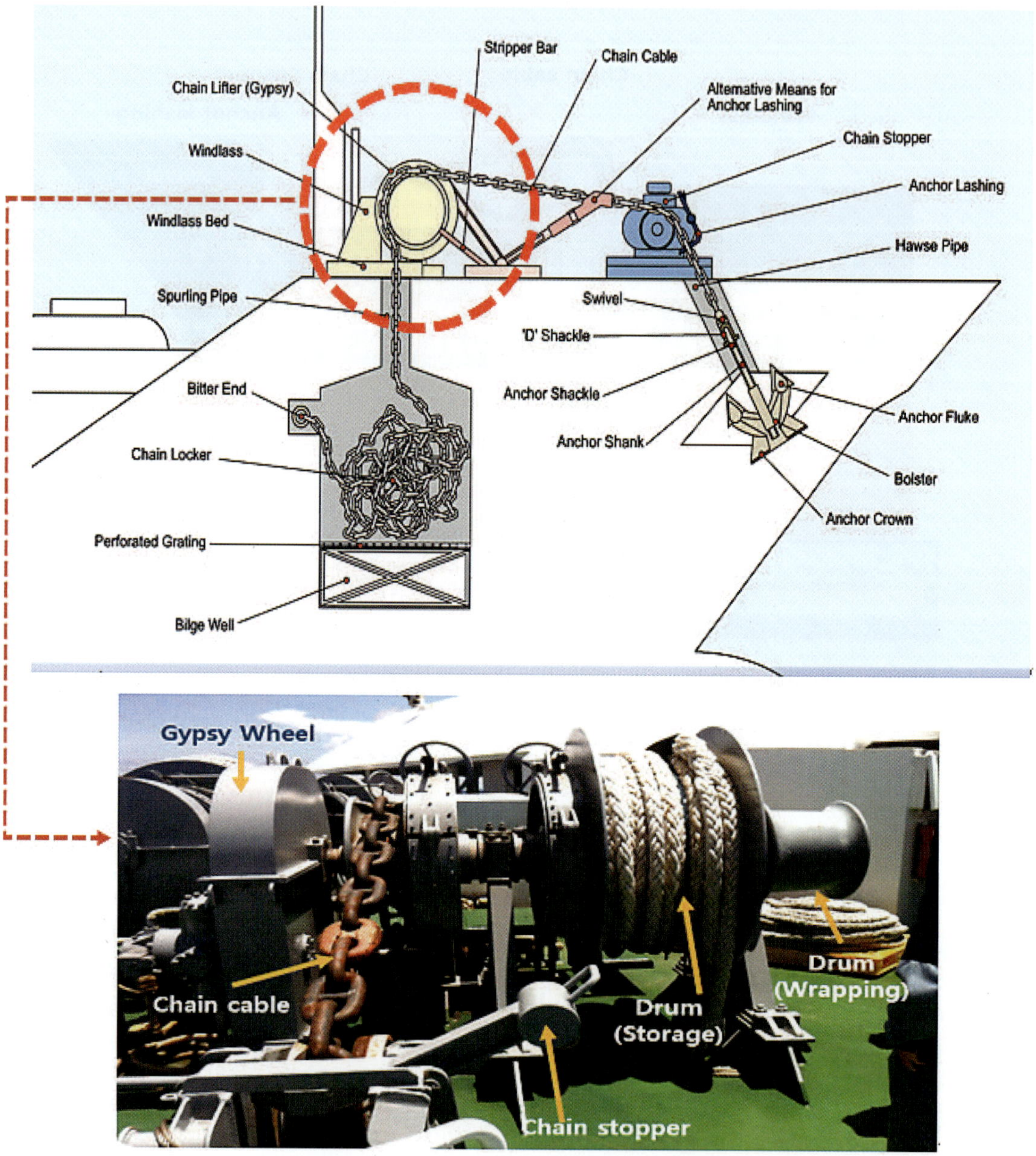

Fig. 4.10 Anchoring system layout Ⅱ

Table 4.5 Terms of anchoring system

Term	Meaning
Windlass	A deck engine used for heaving in ground tackle or to warp a ship in a ship.
Shackle	A shackle is a device used as a connecting link in rigging systems. A shackle is a unit of length and equal to 27.5 m and is the standard length of a anchor chain.
Chain locker	The compartment in the bow in which the anchor chain is stowed.

4.7.4 Anchoring communication phrases

- **Stan-by port / starboard anchor**

- **Let go, anchor**

  The principle followed in this method is to let go or let the anchor slip with cable under its weight from the hawse pipe. The weight on the cable, windlass brake holding power and momentum of a ship are factors to be controlled by the vessel to ensure the anchor digs in, and the cable is subsequently laid to extend backwards.

- **Heave up**

- **Walk back**

  Walking back means lowering the anchor with gear. The principle difference between the walk back and let go methods is that we lower the anchor under power in the walk back.

- **Cock-bill**

  When the anchor is hanging vertically from the hawse pipe, the flukes turn into the ship's side.

- **Up & down anchor**

  The cable is said to be up & down when the angle the cable makes with the water surface is 90°, usually, just before anchor a weigh.

- **Cable leading**

- **Brought up anchor**

  The vessel is said to be brought up when a ship starts to ride the anchor after the anchor has been let go and the required amount of cable is paid out. This is determined when the vessel is heading into the tide, current or wind, and the anchor cable has come to a short stay.

- **Short stay**

  When the anchor cable is leading close to vertical, then the anchor is said to be at a short stay.

- **Long stay**

  When the anchor cable is leading at acute angles, the anchor is said to be at a long stay.

- **Cable slack**

- **Anchor aweigh**

  The anchor is said to be aweigh immediately. It is clear from the bottom.

- **Foul anchor**

  This is the term used to describe the anchor when caught on an underwater obstruction. The anchor's flukes often get fouled by an old hawser or cable.

  - Anchor dragging: The anchor is dragging when it is not held seabed.

4.7.5 Mooring equipment

The term 'mooring' refers to the system for securing a ship to a terminal. The use of an efficient mooring system is essential for the ship's safety, crew, terminal, and environment. The moorings of a ship must resist the forces due to some, or possibly all, of the following factors; wind, current, tides, surges from passing ships, waves / swell / seiche, ice, and changes in draft, trim or list.

Fig. 4.11 Mooring equipment in forecastle

Table 4.6 Terms of mooring equipment

Term	Meaning
Bitts	Bitts are double bollards / posts mounted vertically on ships to secure mooring lines from other vessels, tug lines or secure Fire Wires on Tankers.
Fairleads	Fairleads have a roller attached to them to guide mooring wires to winches for the correct lead.
Winch	An engine mounted on deck and fitted with one or more drums or gipsies for hauling cable, chain, and so on.
Chocks	Chocks are structural reinforcements on ships which guide the mooring lines to and from the shore / other ships.
Bollard	Bollards are generally referred to short posts on the quay / jetty used to secure Ship's Mooring Lines. A single bitt on ships may also be referred to as a bollard around which the eye of the rope is attached.

4.7.6 Mooring arrangement

The term 'mooring pattern' refers to the geometric arrangement of mooring lines between the ship and the berth. It should be noted that the industry has previously standardized the concept of a generic mooring layout, taking into account standard environment criteria. The generic mooring layout is mainly applicable to a 'multi-directional' environment and the design of the ship's mooring equipment.

Fig. 4.12 Mooring arrangement of oil tanker

Table 4.7 Terms of mooring arrangement

Term	Meaning
Mooring	A berth or anchorage in which a vessel is made fast.
Spring line	Docking line led at an angle from the fore-and-aft lines of a vessel. Spring lines are used to keep a ship from going either forward or aft, depending on the lead of the spring lines.
Breast line	Breast lines are led perpendicular to the keel.
Stern line	A line that is led aft from a ship's transom to a piling, cleat, or bollard.
Head line	A mooring line secured forward of the ship's pivot point.

Exercise

Chapter.4

1. Write down key words in this chapter.

2. Summarize the content in this chapter.

✓ **Speed Quiz** – Explain the meaning of the word and Answer the word

ex) Draft	Sheer			

✓ **Speed Quiz** – Explain the meaning of the word and Answer the word

ex) Laden				

✍ Practice Ⅰ

1. Image the word

2. Make the sentence

3. Make your team and story

4. Set the role

5. Presentation with video recording

6. Self-evaluation

7. Feedback

Presentation Evaluation sheet

Team Presenter ____

Title ____

1. Topic clear

1	2	3	4	5	6	7	8	9	10

2. Voice clearance

1	2	3	4	5	6	7	8	9	10

3. Presentation Material

1	2	3	4	5	6	7	8	9	10

4. Maritime Word

1	2	3	4	5	6	7	8	9	10

5. Grammar

1	2	3	4	5	6	7	8	9	10

6. Expression (Body language)

1	2	3	4	5	6	7	8	9	10

7. pace

1	2	3	4	5	6	7	8	9	10

8. story structure

1	2	3	4	5	6	7	8	9	10

9. Q & A

1	2	3	4	5	6	7	8	9	10

10. Overall score

1	2	3	4	5	6	7	8	9	10

✓ **Feedback opinion**

Date ______________

Evaluator ______________

5

Engine System

The main functions of the engine system are divided into the main engine system for propulsion of the ship, the power generation system that supplies electric power to the electric devices, and the boiler that makes heat sources for fuel, lubricating oil and accommodation. In addition, the cargo handling equipment systems according to the type of ship are different. The air conditioning and refrigeration systems that allow crew members to live on the ship are composed of the engine system.

- Main engine for propulsion power
- Generator engine for electric power
- Boiler for steam energy

The figure below shows the main engine and generator's fuel oil system among the engine room pipelines. Tank for fuel storage, pump for fuel supply, steam heater for fuel preheating, purifier, filter, valve, pipeline, temperature and pressure indicator are required. A single device cannot perform its functions, so the help of various auxiliary machinery is required.

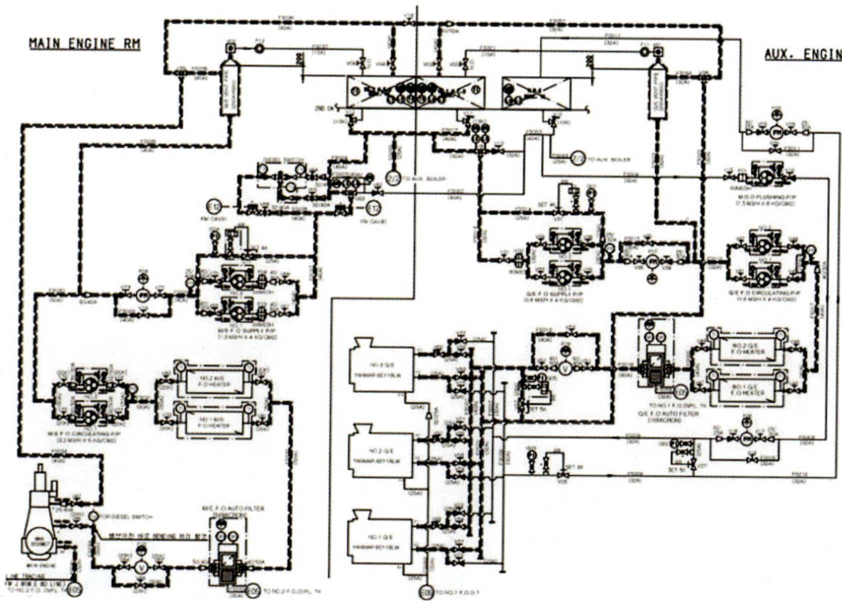

Fig. 5.1 Fuel piping diagram for main engine and generator engine

In the case of the above-mentioned main engine, generator, and boiler, scavenge air for combustion should be supplied to generate necessary engine power, electric power, and heat energy using fuel. In the case of an engine, a supply of lubricating oil for operation and cooling fresh water is required, and a control system, alarm and monitoring system are required.

- Scavenge air system
- Fuel oil system
- Lubricating oil system
- Cooling fresh water system
- Control air and starting air supply system
- Control and Monitoring system

5.1 Main Engine & Shaft

The main engine can be divided into three structures; the bed plate, which is the lowest part, the frame box with the driving part, and the cylinder frame with the combustion chamber. The governor system that controls the fuel amount and injection timing according to commands from the bridge or engine control room adjust the engine speed. The injected fuel reacts with the air supplied by the turbocharger in the combustion chamber and transfers the explosive energy to the piston crown in the cylinder liner. Furthermore, the crankshaft rotates, and this rotational force is transmitted to the propeller through the shaft.

Fig. 5.2 Cylinder frame, frame box, bed plate of main engine

In the case of a shaft system, it has a different shaft system depending on the ship's length. It is composed of an intermediate shaft in the case of a long shaft starting from the engine's crankshaft and a tail shaft connected to the propeller.

Fig. 5.3 Intermediate shaft and bearing

5.2 Generator Engine

In the case of the power generation system, it is a crucial system that supplies the power source for the ship. Except for the main engine, generator, boiler and incinerator that directly burns fuel in the combustion chamber, other machinery and cargo handling equipment use electric power as an energy source. Electric motors also generate hydraulic power for the hydraulic power system. In addition, the navigation equipment also uses electricity, so if the electric power is lost, such as in the black out case, the ship's operation is impossible. Three or more generators are installed on merchant ships to prepare for this emergency.

Fig. 5.4 Generator engine

If there is a problem with the generator, a standby generator is automatically started, and if it also fails, the system gives an order to run the emergency generator.

In the operation of the generator, like the main engine, it has the fuel oil supply system, scavenge air supply system, lubricant supply system, cooling system, control system, alarm and monitoring system. In order to supply the electric power, a system for synchronizing the power generated by each generator through the main switchboard is arranged.

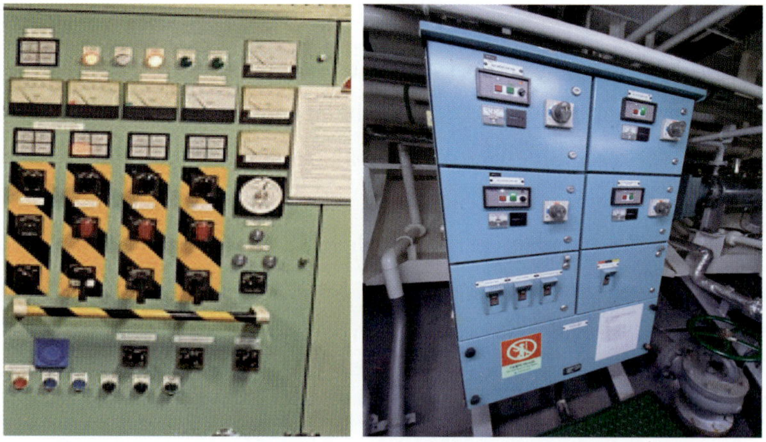

Fig. 5.5 Synchronizing panel and local group starter panel

5.3 Auxiliary Boiler

The fuel for marine machinery, low - cost oil, has a very high viscosity, so heating by a heat source is required to adjust the viscosity to a suitable viscosity for combustion. In addition, in the case of fuel oil and lubricating oil, continuous cleaning is required, and even during cleaning, a heat source is required to satisfy a specific viscosity through heating. In the case of a vessel operating in the polar regions, temperature control of the accommodation is required. Even in the case of a vessel leaving after docking repair, such a heat source is required for engine warming.

In the case of a boiler system, its configuration is simple compared with an engine system. It consists of a fuel supply system, air supply system, control system and alarm system. The fuel energy burned in the furnace with air is heated in the water drum and rises through the tube to the steam drum. The generated steam is delivered to the heater required for cooling the engine room, and the cooled steam heat - exchanged goes through the dump condenser to the cascade tank. The condensed water is re-supplied to the boiler through the boiler water circulation pump.

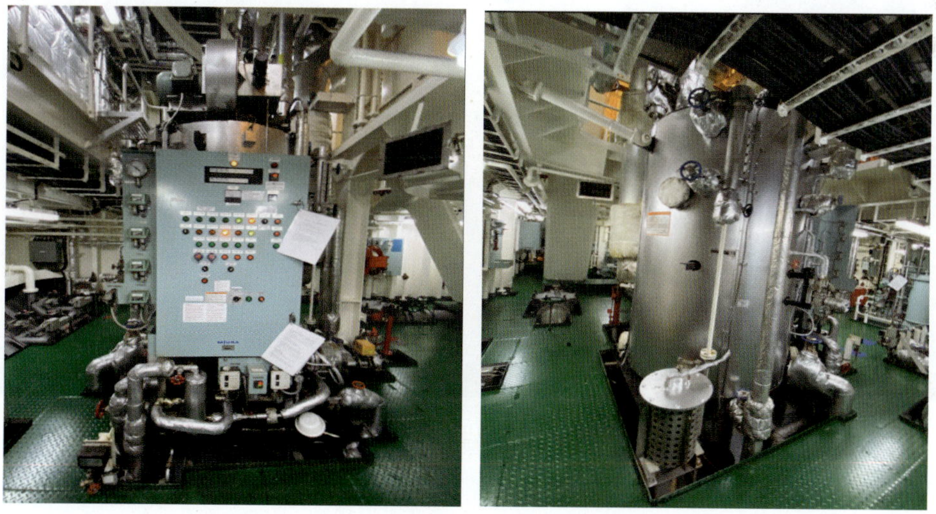

Fig. 5.6 Auxiliary boiler

5.4 Auxiliary and Machineries

Various devices and facilities exist in the engine room, depending on the purpose of use and the type of fluid. Most fluid supply devices such as fuel oil, lubricating oil, freshwater, and seawater are supplied by a pump driven by an electric motor. A hydraulic motor and hydraulic power pack are used to supply hydraulic pressure. In the case of air, a compressor is used, and when heating a heat source to control the temperature of the fluid, a cooler is used to cool the heater. A purifier, strainer, and filter are used to clean fuel oil or lubricating oil.

In order to treat other wastes and engine room bilge water, an incinerator, an oily water separator, and a sewage treatment system are installed to treat sewage in the ship.

Fig. 5.7 Pump and motor

Fig. 5.8 Purifier room

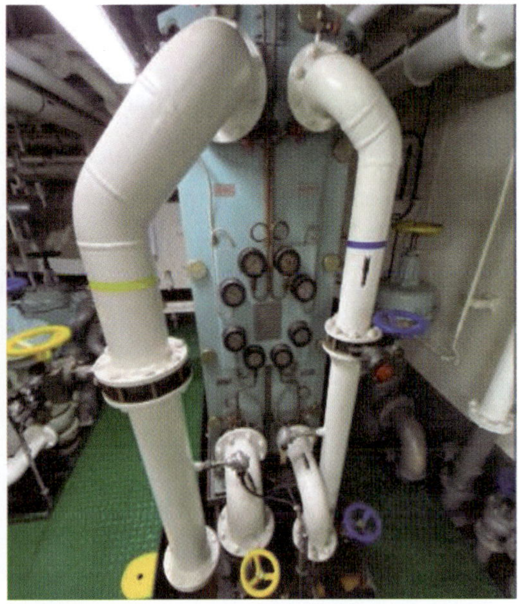

Fig. 5.9 Cooler

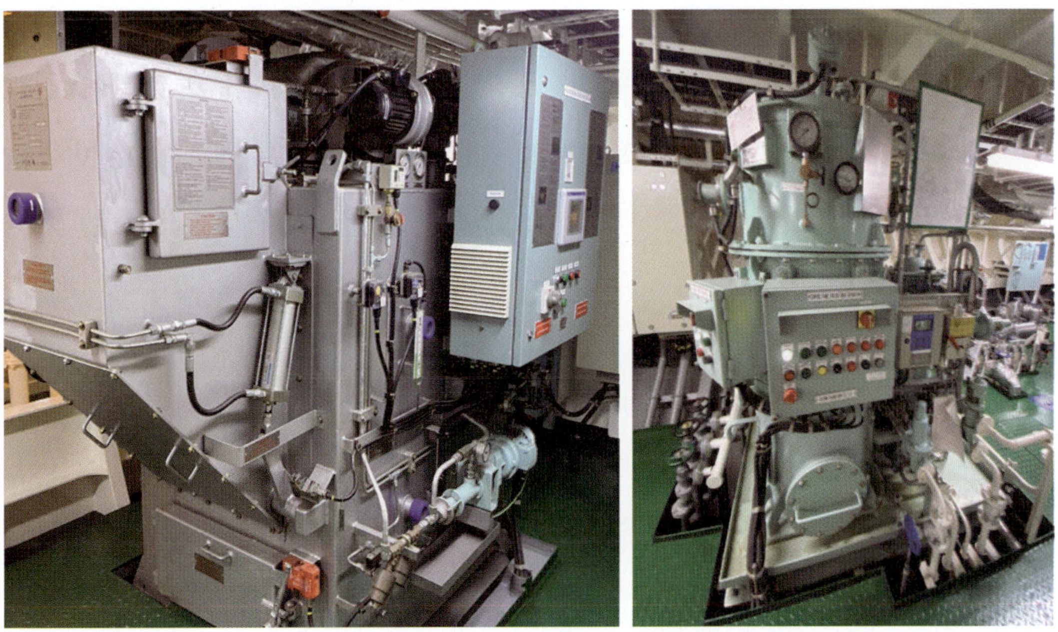

Fig. 5.10 Incinerator and oily water separator

5.5 Pipe Line

In order to understand the engine system of a ship, it is essential to understand not only the structure, operation and maintenance of each piece of equipment but also the system configuration related to the equipment. Since these systems are physically connected through pipelines, the movement of fluids through pipelines must be understood. Fluids use separate pipelines. The types of fluids are as follows, and they have a particular colour for classification.

■ Sea water
■ Fresh water
■ Lubricating oil
■ Fuel oil
■ Steam and condensed water
□ Compressed air
■ Oily Bilge water
■ Exhaust air

Applicable machinery and system related to the pipeline can be classified as follows.

- Main engine
- Generator engine
- Auxiliaries
- Safety system (Fire, Quick closing valve system)

In addition, the symbols of various valves, instrumentation lines, and various facilities are specified on the pipeline. The pipeline starts with the tank, a storage container, then passes through the pump with the connected valve and is supplied to the machinery and system.

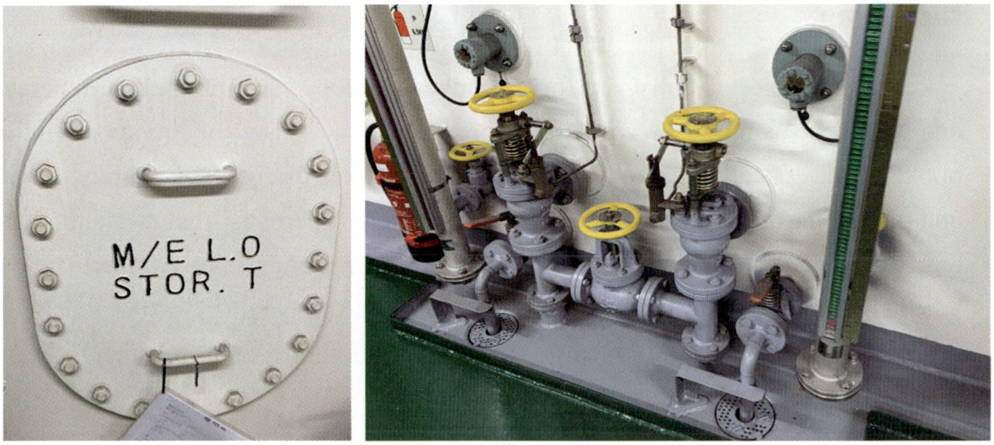

Fig. 5.11 Tank and valve

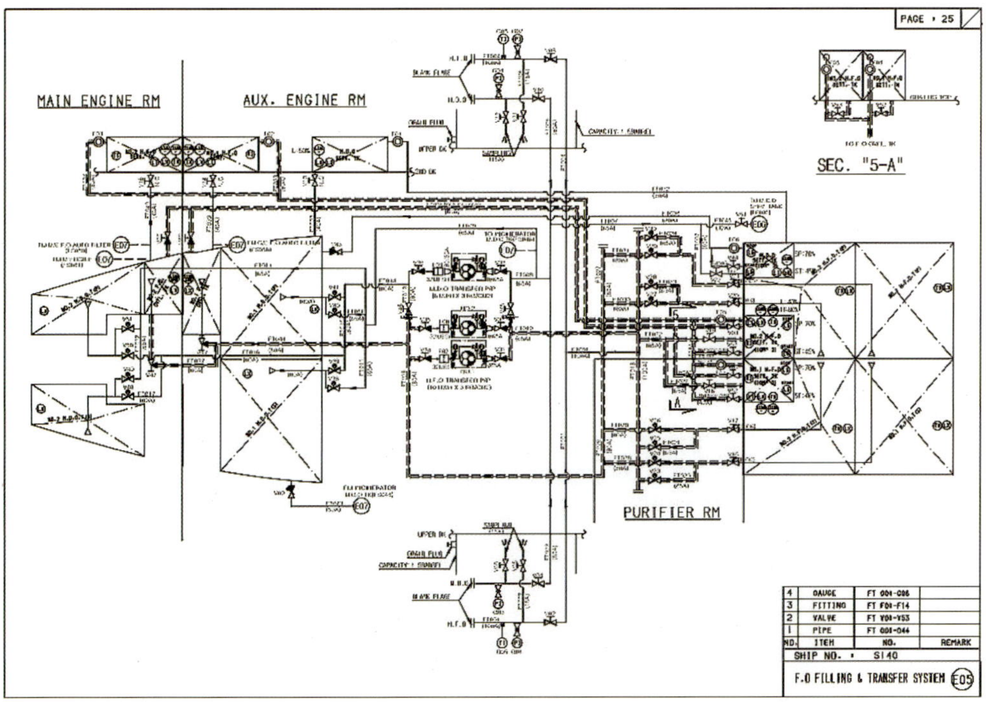

Fig. 5.12 F.O. filling and transfer system pipe line

5.6 Bunkering

Ships must periodically perform bunkering for main engines, generators, and boilers using fuel for operation. In the case of merchant ships, bunkering is usually carried out so that a bunker barge is berthing the ship and supplying the fuel. The point to be noted here is that watchers must pay attention to whether the bunker supply matches the contract amount, whether the bunker supply is being supplied safely due to the change in draft caused by waves and cargo handling operations, and whether oil spills due to pipeline leakage.

- Check the R.O.B(Remain On Board) of the bunker oil tank of a ship through sounding
- Check the R.O.B. bunker oil tank of the barge
- Check bunker oil specification documents
- Check the connection of the bunkering line and prepare for oil sampling
- Commence bunkering according to telecommunication
- Keep watching the condition on the site
- Finish bunkering
- Check the R.O.B. of the ship by sounding
- Check the R.O.B. of bunkers on the side of the barge
- Signing the paperwork
- Disconnect bunkering hose

Fig. 5.13 Bunkering

Exercise

Chapter.5

1. Write down key words in this chapter.

2. Summarize the content in this chapter.

✓ **Speed Quiz** – Explain the function of machinery and Answer the word

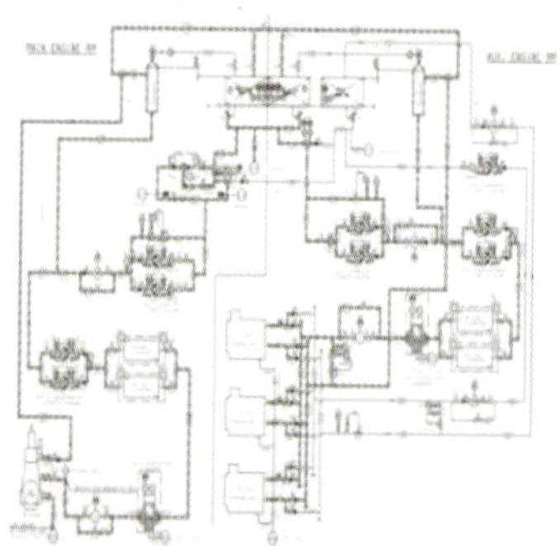

✓ **Speed Quiz** – Explain the function of machinery and Answer the word

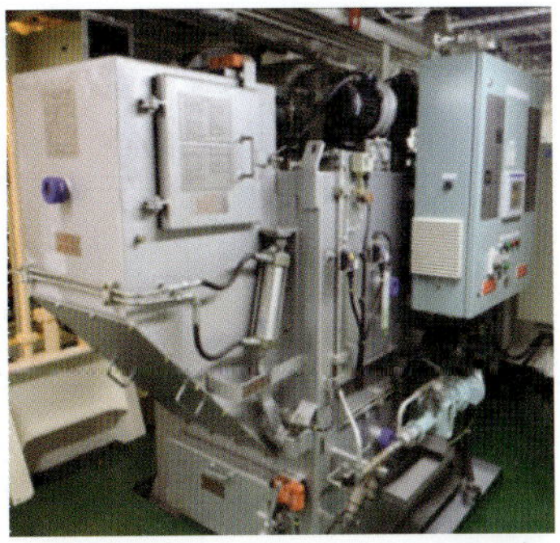

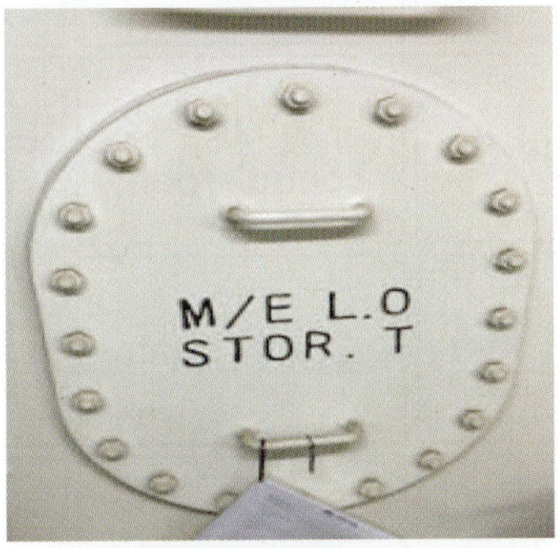

✓ **Speed Quiz** – Explain the meaning of the word and Answer the word

Main engine	Propulsion	Generator engine	Boiler	Lubricating oil
Refrigeration system	Accommodati on	Cargo handling	Fuel oil	Auxiliary machineries
Tank	Heater	Purifier	Filter	Valve
Pipeline	Temperature	Pressure	Scavenge air	Combustion
Control system	Alarm	Monitoring system	Starting air supply system	Shaft
Bed plate	Frame box	Cylinder frame	Governor	Injection timing
Bridge	Engine control room	Engine speed	Turbocharger	Piston crown
Cylinder liner	Crank shaft	Propeller	Intermediate shaft	Crankshaft
Bearing	Incinerator	Hydraulic power	Navigation	Equipment
Black out	Emergency	Merchant ships	Cooling system	Main switch board
Starter panel	Synchronizing panel	Local group starter panel	Viscosity	Polar

✓ **Speed Quiz** – Explain the meaning of the word and Answer the word

Docking repair	Engine warming	Furnace	Water drum	Steam drum
Dump condenser	Cascade tank	Boiler water circulation pump	Hydraulic power pack	Hydraulic pressure compressor
Compressor	Strainer	Bilge water	Oily water separator	Sewage treatment system
Operation	Maintenance	Equipment	Sea water	Fresh water
Exhaust air	Safety system	Quick closing valve system	Instrumentati on line	Bunkering
Draft	Leakage.	R.O.B	Sounding	Barge
Specification	Oil sampling	Telecommuni cation	Finish	

✍ Practice Ⅰ

1. Image the word

2. Make the sentence

3. Make your team and story

4. Set the role

5. Presentation with video recording

6. Self-evaluation

7. Feedback

Presentation Evaluation sheet

Team Presenter ______

Title ______

1. Topic clear

1	2	3	4	5	6	7	8	9	10

2. Voice clearance

1	2	3	4	5	6	7	8	9	10

3. Presentation Material

1	2	3	4	5	6	7	8	9	10

4. Maritime Word

1	2	3	4	5	6	7	8	9	10

5. Grammar

1	2	3	4	5	6	7	8	9	10

6. Expression (Body language)

1	2	3	4	5	6	7	8	9	10

7. pace

1	2	3	4	5	6	7	8	9	10

8. story structure

1	2	3	4	5	6	7	8	9	10

9. Q & A

1	2	3	4	5	6	7	8	9	10

10. Overall score

1	2	3	4	5	6	7	8	9	10

✓ **Feedback opinion**

Date ______________

Evaluator ______________

✍ Practice Ⅱ

1. Image the word

2. Make the sentence

3. Make your team and story

4. Set the role

5. Presentation with video recording

6. Self-evaluation

7. Feedback

Presentation Evaluation sheet

Team Presenter ________

Title ________

1. Topic clear

1	2	3	4	5	6	7	8	9	10

2. Voice clearance

1	2	3	4	5	6	7	8	9	10

3. Presentation Material

1	2	3	4	5	6	7	8	9	10

4. Maritime Word

1	2	3	4	5	6	7	8	9	10

5. Grammar

1	2	3	4	5	6	7	8	9	10

6. Expression (Body language)

1	2	3	4	5	6	7	8	9	10

7. pace

1	2	3	4	5	6	7	8	9	10

8. story structure

1	2	3	4	5	6	7	8	9	10

9. Q & A

1	2	3	4	5	6	7	8	9	10

10. Overall score

1	2	3	4	5	6	7	8	9	10

✓ **Feedback opinion**

Date ____________ Evaluator ____________

✍ Practice Ⅲ

1. Image the word

2. Make the sentence

3. Make your team and story

4. Set the role

5. Presentation with video recording

6. Self-evaluation

7. Feedback

Presentation Evaluation sheet

Team Presenter

Title

1. Topic clear

1	2	3	4	5	6	7	8	9	10

2. Voice clearance

1	2	3	4	5	6	7	8	9	10

3. Presentation Material

1	2	3	4	5	6	7	8	9	10

4. Maritime Word

1	2	3	4	5	6	7	8	9	10

5. Grammar

1	2	3	4	5	6	7	8	9	10

6. Expression (Body language)

1	2	3	4	5	6	7	8	9	10

7. pace

1	2	3	4	5	6	7	8	9	10

8. story structure

1	2	3	4	5	6	7	8	9	10

9. Q & A

1	2	3	4	5	6	7	8	9	10

10. Overall score

1	2	3	4	5	6	7	8	9	10

✓ **Feedback opinion**

Date ______________ Evaluator ______________

✍ Practice Ⅳ

1. Image the word

2. Make the sentence

3. Make your team and story

4. Set the role

5. Presentation with video recording

6. Self-evaluation

7. Feedback

Presentation Evaluation sheet

Team Presenter

Title

1. Topic clear

1	2	3	4	5	6	7	8	9	10

2. Voice clearance

1	2	3	4	5	6	7	8	9	10

3. Presentation Material

1	2	3	4	5	6	7	8	9	10

4. Maritime Word

1	2	3	4	5	6	7	8	9	10

5. Grammar

1	2	3	4	5	6	7	8	9	10

6. Expression (Body language)

1	2	3	4	5	6	7	8	9	10

7. pace

1	2	3	4	5	6	7	8	9	10

8. story structure

1	2	3	4	5	6	7	8	9	10

9. Q & A

1	2	3	4	5	6	7	8	9	10

10. Overall score

1	2	3	4	5	6	7	8	9	10

✓ **Feedback opinion**

Date ____________

Evaluator ____________

6

Cargo

6.1 Cargo Operation
6.2 Cargo Gear
6.3 Ballast and Deballast
6.4 Ship's Stability

6.1 Cargo Operation

A cargo ship or freighter is a merchant ship that carries cargo, goods and materials from one port to another. Thousands of cargo carriers ply the world's seas and oceans each year, handling the bulk of international trade. Cargo ships are usually specially designed for the task, often equipped with cranes and other mechanisms to load and unload, and come in all sizes. Today, they are almost always built of welded steel and, with some exceptions, generally have a life expectancy of 25 to 30 years before being scrapped. Technically, "cargo" refers to the goods carried aboard the ship for hire, while "freight" refers to the act of carrying such cargo, but the terms have been used interchangeably for centuries. Cargo ships/freighters can be divided into seven groups according to their cargo type. These groups are shown in the following figure.

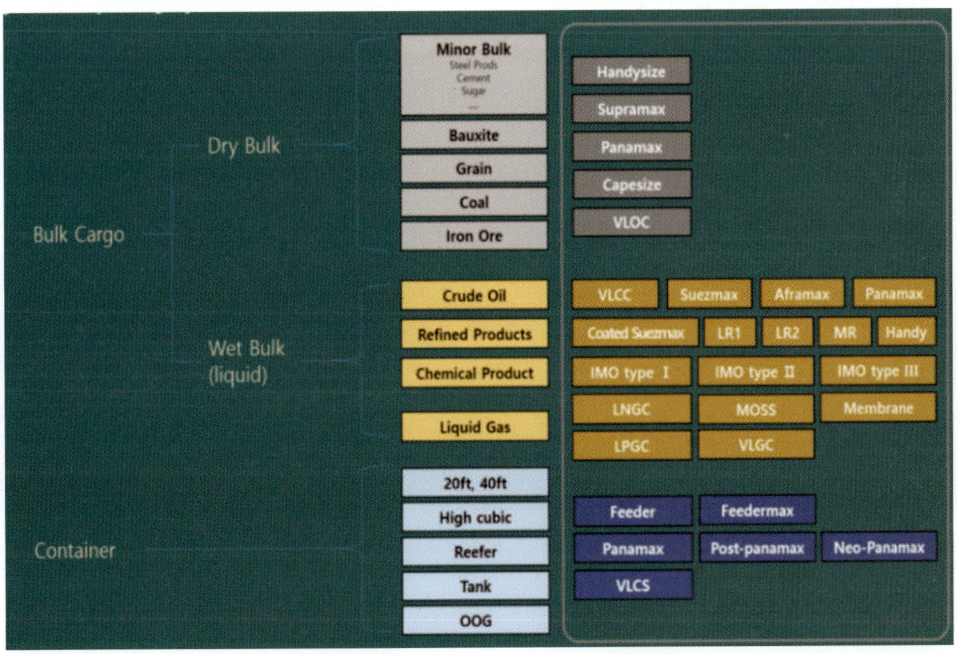

Fig. 6.1 Ship's type by cargoes

Cargo ships are categorized partly by cargo capacity, partly by weight (deadweight tonnage, DWT), and partly by dimensions. Maximum dimensions such as length and width (beam) limit the canal locks a ship can fit in, water depth (draft) is a limitation for canals, shallow straits or harbours, and height limits passing under bridges.

6.2 Cargo Gear

Cargo gear is the cargo handling equipment used for loading and discharging operation: e.g. cargo cranes, a side - loading system with conveyors, side shifters, elevators, belt conveyors, ro-ro cargo handling gear and cargo pumping systems.

6.2.1 Dry bulk cargo gear

Fig. 6.2 Dry bulk terminal : coal

Fig. 6.3 Dry bulk cargo handling gears

Cargo handling equipment varies depending upon the type of cargo. Oil tankers are fitted with pumping systems and pumps, small cranes to handle shore hoses, tank cleaning machines and inert-gas generating systems. Most dry - bulk carriers depend on shoreside facilities for cargo loading and discharge. However, some bulk carriers have self-unloading features with conveyors below cargo holds or cranes on deck. Reefer vessels are designed with refrigerated cargo holds fitted with large cargo-refrigeration systems.

6.2.2 Container cargo gear

Fig. 6.4 Container terminal

Fig. 6.5 Container handling gears

6.2.3 Tanker cargo gear

Fig. 6.6 Cargo operation of oil tanker

Fig. 6.7 LNG Terminal operation

6.3 Ballast and Deballast

Ballasting or de-ballasting is a process by which seawater is taken in and out of the ship when the ship is at the port or sea. The seawater carried by ship is known as ballast water. Ballast water is generally seawater carried by vessel (ship) in its ballast tanks to ensure its trim, stability and structural integrity.

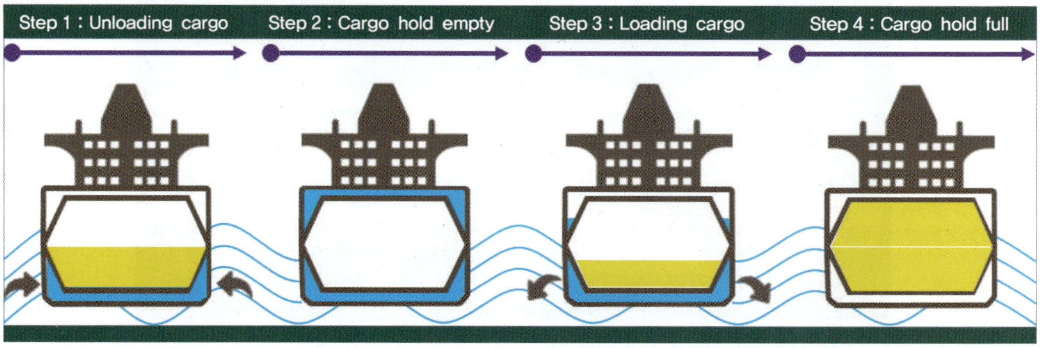

Fig. 6.8 Ballasting and deballasting

- **Step 1** : Ballast water pumped into ship at unloading port (Ballasting)
- **Step 2** : Ship sails with full ballast tank (Ballast voyage)
- **Step 3** : Ballast water discharged at loading port (Deballasting)
- **Step 4** : Ship sails with empty tank (Laden voyage)

Ballast tanks are constructed in ships with a piping system, and high capacity ballast pumps to carry out the operation. When no cargo is carried by ship, the latter becomes light in weight, affecting its stability. For this reason, ballast water is taken into dedicated tanks in the ship to stabilize it. Tanks are filled with ballast water with the help of high capacity ballast pumps, and this process is known as Ballasting. However, when the ship is filled with cargo, the ship's stability is maintained by the weight of the cargo itself, and thus there is no ballast water requirement. Taking out ballast water from the ballast tanks to make them empty is known as de-ballasting.

6.4 Ship's Stability

Ship stability is an area of naval architecture and ship design that deals with how a ship behaves at sea, both in still water and in waves, whether intact or damaged. Stability calculations focus on centers of gravity, centers of buoyancy, the metacenters of vessels, and on how these interact.

6.4.1 Plimsol mark (= load line)

The purpose of a load line is to ensure that a ship has sufficient freeboard (the height from the water line to the main deck) and thus sufficient reserve buoyancy.

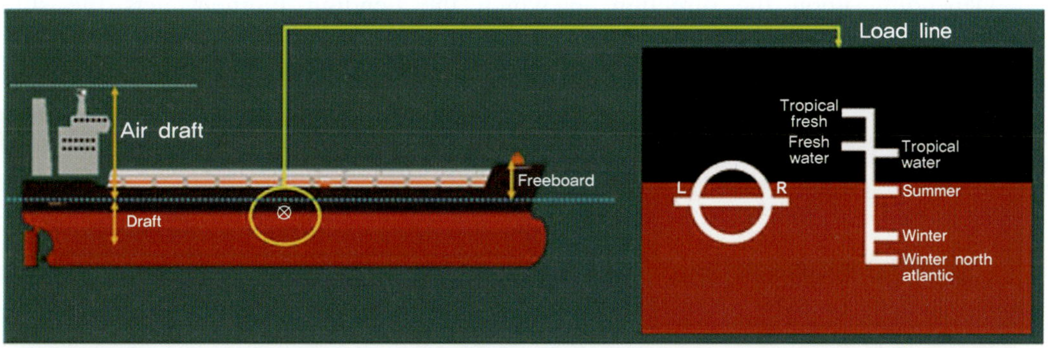

Fig. 6.9 Load line

▼**Table 6.1** Terms of load line

Term	Meaning
Draft (draught)	The depth of water required to float a vessel; the navigational draft is the distance from the actual waterline to the bottom of the keel.
Freeboard	The vertical distance from the waterline to the upper deck; usually measured amidships.
Air draft	The distance from the waterline to the highest point on a ship.
Plimsol mark	The figure on the side of a merchant ship that shows the various draft levels to which a ship may be loaded, depending on the region and season in which a vessel is scheduled to sail.

6.4.2 Hull stress : hog, sag, trim, heel

Modern ship is made up of steel plating, sections and builds up girders to provide adequate strength in all parts to withstand the forces acting on the ship under all conditions of service. The forces acting on a ship may be static or dynamic. The static forces are due to the difference in the weight and buoyancy, which occur throughout the ship. The dynamic forces are caused by the motion of the ship at sea and the action of the wind and wave. These forces create longitudinal stress, transverse stress, and local stress. The greatest stress set in the ship as wholes are due to the distribution of load along with the ship, causing longitudinal bending. The forces are two in number, the weight of the ship and all that it carries acting downwards and the vertical component of the hydrostatic pressure. Depending upon the direction in which the bending moment acts the ship will Hog or Sag.

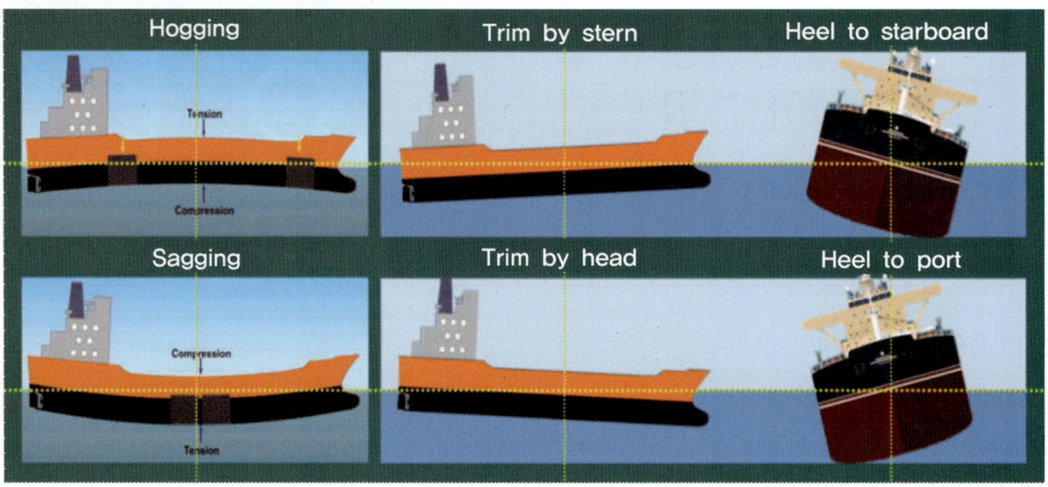

Fig. 6.10 Hull stress

▼**Table 6.2** Terms of hull stress

Term	Meaning
Hogging	The tendency of a ship to arch up amidships as the result of improper weight distribution.
Sagging	The longitudinal deformation that occurs under a stress that causes the waist of a vessel to drop below the bow and stern.
Trim	The difference of the drafts between forward and aft.
Heel	A temporary transverse angle of inclination of a vessel to one side or the other such as during a roll or caused by the wind.
List	A transverse angle of inclination caused by internal forces.

Exercise

Chapter.6

1. Write down key words in this chapter.

2. Summarize the content in this chapter.

Record & Listen your voice reading the sentence

✓ **Speed Quiz** – Explain the meaning of the word and Answer the word

✍ Plactice

1. Image the word

2. Make the sentence

3. Make your team and story

4. Set the role

5. Presentation with video recording

6. Self-evaluation

7. Feedback

Record & Listen your voice reading the sentence

Presentation Evaluation sheet

Team Presenter

Title

1. Topic clear

1	2	3	4	5	6	7	8	9	10

2. Voice clearance

1	2	3	4	5	6	7	8	9	10

3. Presentation Material

1	2	3	4	5	6	7	8	9	10

4. Maritime Word

1	2	3	4	5	6	7	8	9	10

5. Grammar

1	2	3	4	5	6	7	8	9	10

6. Expression (Body language)

1	2	3	4	5	6	7	8	9	10

7. pace

1	2	3	4	5	6	7	8	9	10

8. story structure

1	2	3	4	5	6	7	8	9	10

9. Q & A

1	2	3	4	5	6	7	8	9	10

10. Overall score

1	2	3	4	5	6	7	8	9	10

✓ Feedback opinion

Date ________________ Evaluator ________________

7

Maneuvering

7.1 Turning Circle
7.2 Speed
7.3 6 Degrees of Motions
7.4 Steering Gear & Operation
7.5 Emergency (Crash Astern, Rough Sea)
7.6 Engine Operation

7.1 Turning Circle

Ship's maneuvering characteristics can be classified as turning, yaw-checking, course-keeping and stopping abilities. Scale model tests and/or computer predictions using mathematical models can be performed to predict the maneuverability of the ships at the design stage. Full-scale maneuvering tests should be conducted to validate these results.

Maneuvering performance has traditionally received little attention during the design stages of a commercial ship. Consequently, some ships have been built with inferior maneuvering qualities that have resulted in marine casualties. "Standards for Ship Maneuverability" were adopted by the IMO resolution MSC.137 (76) in December 2002 to ensure that ships are designed to a uniform standard.

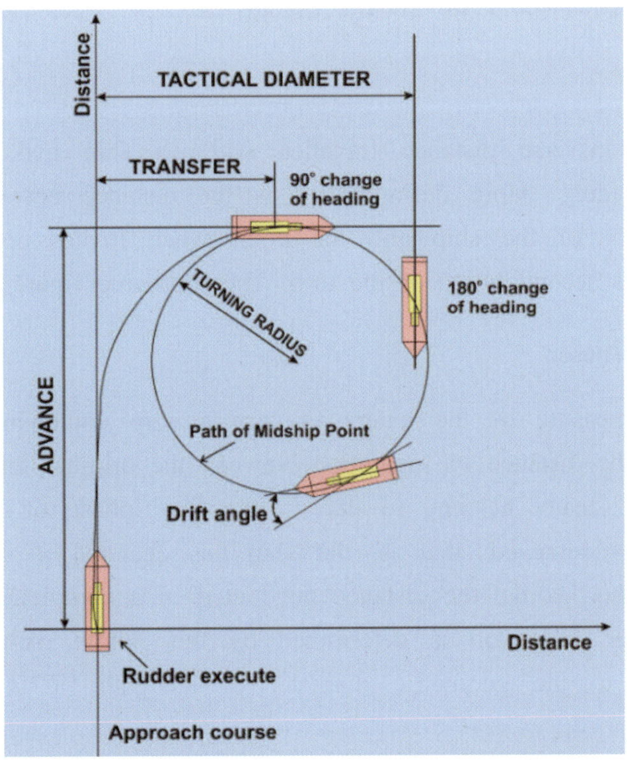

Fig. 7.1 Terms and concept of turning circle

The aim of performing this trial is to test the ship's overall 'Turning Ability' as it comprises an indispensable maneuver that a ship has to undergo every now and then. Following are some of the outcomes that were chiefly recorded and assessed while conducting this trial:

7.1.1 Advance

Advance is the distance surged by the ship forward after the rudder angle is applied. As mentioned earlier, a ship has to manifest all the hydrodynamic effects associated with it while performing any change in its motion. Unlike a car, it cannot just turn right away after applying the rudder deviation. After traversing some distance, it gradually does so. However, proper sea-handling characteristics demand a faster response to an operator order. Though no hard and fast rules exist, for a given ship type and speed, a minimal advance criteria are always sought.

7.1.2 Transfer

It is the transverse distance travelled while a ship makes a 90 - degree change in heading. More definitely, it is the distance between the original direction vector of the ship and the point when it has completely headed starboard in its second phase of the turn. The following figure illustrates better.

7.1.3 Tactical diameter

This is a measure of the extent of turn a ship could have. Thus, it is measured as the distance of separation between the original direction vector of the ship at a steady heading to that in the final phase of its turn when a steady state is achieved, that is, the ship has changed its heading by 180 degrees. In other words, the distance negotiated in a complete turnaround at a constant rudder deflection is determined by this length. As the distance is almost equal to the geometric diameter of its path, it is called Tactical Diameter.

7.2 Speed

There are various terms to describe speed in ship maneuvering. It uses "Ahead" and "Astern" to indicate the ship's direction with "PORT" and "Starboard (STBD)" including angle. To give an order for the amount speed rate, it uses "Nav. Full", "Full", "Half", "Slow", "Dead Slow", Etc. When the engine is stopped, it uses "Stop Engine", and in case of an urgent situation, "Emergency" is used.

In addition, "Stand by Engine" requests are made from the bridge to the engine control room, and after engine use is finished, use the expression "Finished with the Engine".

Table 7.1 Standard ship engine orders

Order
Nav. Full ahead
Full ahead
Half ahead
Slow ahead
Dead slow ahead
Stop engine
Dead slow astern
Slow astern
Half astern
Full astern
Nav. Full astern
Emergency full ahead / astern
Stand by engine
Finished with engine

In ships with bow thruster or stern thruster, the terms are similar to using a telegraph; the degree of speed with ship direction are used together.

Table 7.2 Standard thruster order

Bow thruster				Stem thruster			
Half	Full	Half	Full	Half	Full	Half	Full
STBD		PORT		STBD		PORT	

7.3 6 Degrees of Motions

Ship motions are defined by the six degrees of freedom (6 - DOF) that a ship can experience.

The vertical (Z - axis), or yaw axis, is an imaginary line running vertically through the ship and through its center of gravity. A yaw motion is a side to side movement of the bow and stern of the ship.

The transverse (Y - axis), lateral axis, or pitch axis is an imaginary line running horizontally across the ship and through the center of gravity. A pitch motion is an up - or - down movement of the bow and stern of the ship.

The longitudinal (X - axis), or roll axis, is an imaginary line running horizontally through the length of the ship, through its center of gravity, and parallel to the waterline. A roll motion is a side - to - side or port - starboard tilting motion of the superstructure around the axis.

- Three degrees of rotation – Angularly moving about the three axes
- Roll – Rotating about the longitudinal horizontal axis is ROLLING
- Pitsh – Rotating about the lateral horizontal axis is PITCHING
- Yaw – Rotating about the vertical axis is YAWING

- Three degrees of freedom – Linearly moving along the three axes
- Surge – Moving forwards and backwards along the longitudinal horizontal axis is called SURGING
- Sway – Moving left and right along the lateral horizontal axis is called SWAYING
- Heave – Moving up and down along the vertical axis is called HEAVING

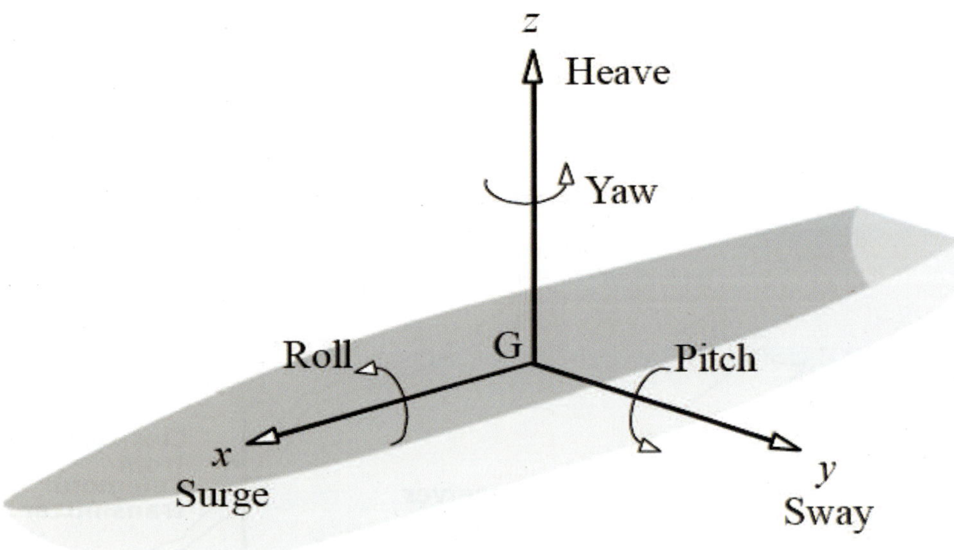

Fig. 7.2 6 Degrees of motions

7.4 Steering Gear & Operation

The steering gear provides a movement of the rudder in response to a signal from the bridge to steer the ship. The direction of a ship moving through the water is controlled by changing the angle of the rudder located in the stern of the ship. As the gross tonnage of the ship increases, more and more force is required to move the rudder through the required angle.

The power required to position the rudder on a large ship is provided by electro-hydraulic steering gear comprising power units, hydraulic rams, and cylinders.

Electrohydraulic steering gear responds to rudder orders transmitted electrically from the helm in the ship's bridge to the steering gear, located directly above the rudder in the stern.

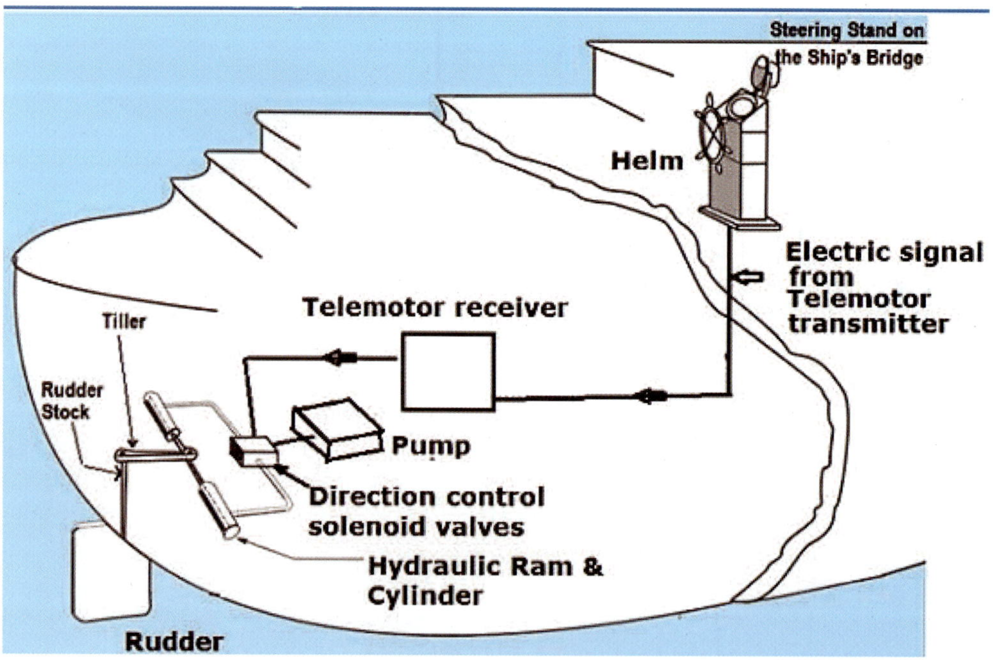

Fig. 7.3 Concept of ship steering system

The art of steering a ship can be gained by practice. The ship's head, rudder, and steering wheel all turn the same way to turn the ship to starboard; one must turn the wheel to starboard. The angle of turn given to the rudder is shown in degrees on the helm indicator situated forward of the wheel.

All orders received by the helmsman are to be repeated twice, once when the order is received and again when the order has been carried out. This ensures that the helmsman has both understood and carried out the orders correctly.

Fig. 7.4 Rudder angle indicator

Fig. 7.5 Streering wheel

Table 7.3 Steering orders

Order	Meaning
Midships	Rubber to be held in the fore and aft position
Port five	5° of Port rudder to be held.
Port ten	10° of Port rudder to be held.
Port fitteen	15° of Port rudder to be held.
Port twenty	20° of Port rudder to be held.
Port twenty-five	25° of Port rudder to be held.
Hard-a-port	Rudder to be held fully over to port.
Stanbord five	5° of starboard rudder to be held.
Stanbord ten	10° of starboard rudder to be held.
Stanbord fifteen	15° of starboard rudder to be held.
Stanbord twenty	20° of starboard rudder to be held.
Stanbord twenty - five	25° of starboard rudder to be held.
Hard-a-starboard	Rudder to be held fully over to port.
Ease to five	Reduce amount of rudder to 5° and hold.
Ease to ten	Reduce amount of rudder to 10° and hold.
Ease to fifteen	Reduce amount of rudder to 15° and hold.
Ease to twenty	Reduce amount of rudder to 20° and hold.
Steady	Reduce swing as rapidly as possible.
Steady as she goes	Steer a steady course on the compass heading indicated at the time of the order. The helmsman is to repeat the order and call out the compass heading on receiving th order. When the ship is stead on the heading, the helsman is to call out: "Steady..."

7.5 Emergency (Crash Estern, Rough Sea)

If crash astern is used for collision prevention and avoidance during ship operation, ship's officer can adjust the maneuvering handle to full astern in the ahead running condition. Then, the fuel is cut off automatically according to the system, and when the revolution per minute(rpm) of the engine is below 20 ~ 25%, braking air is supplied to stop the engine, and astern enters when the engine is stopped. After that, the speed automatically increases until full astern. This is not to stop and use astern sequentially according to the navigator's order in emergencies during sailing but to automatically enter the astern command by the system. Electric propulsion ships also have this function, and when the rpm drops to 40%, braking is applied, and a faster reversal can be achieved.

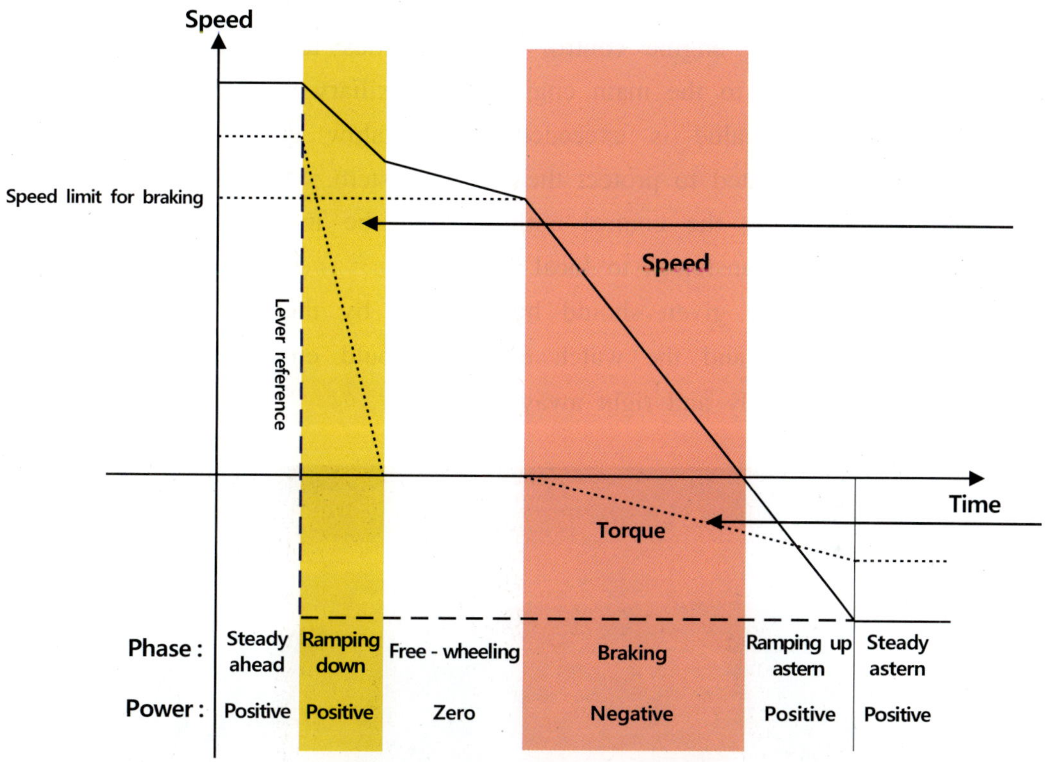

Fig. 7.6 Crash astern sequence

Among the rpm control mode and torque mode, the rpm control mode is mainly used in the rough sea, and the fuel index is followed according to the user's rpm command to supplement the fuel index. When the engine rpm changes rapidly, the rpm control is mainly performed to prevent the engine from being stopped due to an over - speed trip, and the turbocharger surging problem may occur due to the load fluctuation, so engineers stand on watch and adjust thc rpm and load.

7.6 Engine Operation

After the engine is warmed up and turned, a test run is performed to check the operation of the engine in the engine control room, and then the authority to control the engine is transferred to the bridge.

The engine can be controlled in the engine control room like the bridge. In addition, in the engine control room, various temperature and pressure information related to the main engine and auxiliary machinery can be read. When the limit value is exceeded, alarm, slow down, and shut down functions are activated to protect the engine system.

In an emergency, the control authority can be transferred to the engine room or directly transferred to local operation.

Any engine order given should be repeated by the person operating the bridge telegraph, and the watch officers should ensure that the order is carried out correctly and right away.

Fig. 7.7 Manevering handle in engine control room

Exercise

Chapter.7

1. Write down key words in this chapter.

2. Summarize the content in this chapter.

✓ **Speed Quiz** – Explain the meaning of the word and Answer the word

✍ Practice Ⅰ

1. Image the word

2. Make the sentence

3. Make your team and story

4. Set the role

5. Presentation with video recording

6. Self-evaluation

7. Feedback

Presentation Evaluation sheet

Team Presenter

Title

1. Topic clear

1	2	3	4	5	6	7	8	9	10

2. Voice clearance

1	2	3	4	5	6	7	8	9	10

3. Presentation Material

1	2	3	4	5	6	7	8	9	10

4. Maritime Word

1	2	3	4	5	6	7	8	9	10

5. Grammar

1	2	3	4	5	6	7	8	9	10

6. Expression (Body language)

1	2	3	4	5	6	7	8	9	10

7. pace

1	2	3	4	5	6	7	8	9	10

8. story structure

1	2	3	4	5	6	7	8	9	10

9. Q & A

1	2	3	4	5	6	7	8	9	10

10. Overall score

1	2	3	4	5	6	7	8	9	10

✓ **Feedback opinion**

Date ______________

Evaluator ______________

8

Navigation & Engine Watch

8.1 Bridge
8.2 Watch Schedule
8.3 Navigation Equipment
8.4 Radio Equipment
8.5 Meteorology
8.6 Engine Room Duty, Patrol, Deadman Alarm

8.1 Bridge

The bridge is a room or platform of a merchant ship from which the ship can be commanded. When a ship is underway, the bridge is manned by an officer of the watch, aided usually by an able seafarer acting as a lookout. During critical maneuvers the captain will be on the bridge, often supported by an officer of the watch, an able seaman on the wheel and sometimes a pilot.

Fig. 8.1 Naviation bridge

Bridge resource management (BRM) uses and coordinates all the skills, knowledge, experience, and resources available to the team to achieve the established goals of safety and efficiency of a voyage or any other safety-critical task. BRM aims to prevent accidents at sea caused by human error.

8.2 Watch Schedule

Bridge watch-keeping is the most critical activity conducted at sea because the watchkeeper's diligence rests on the safety and security of the ship, her entire crew and the cargo. It is a demanding activity that requires support, encouragement, motivation, self-discipline and a high standard of professionalism. Ships masters must ensure that all watch-keepers understand the use of safety-related equipment before keeping a watch.

Fig. 8.2 Navigation watch

The system of watch - keeping may differ from ship to ship, but the system usually employed is based upon a three watch rotation, i.e. four hours on and eight hours off.

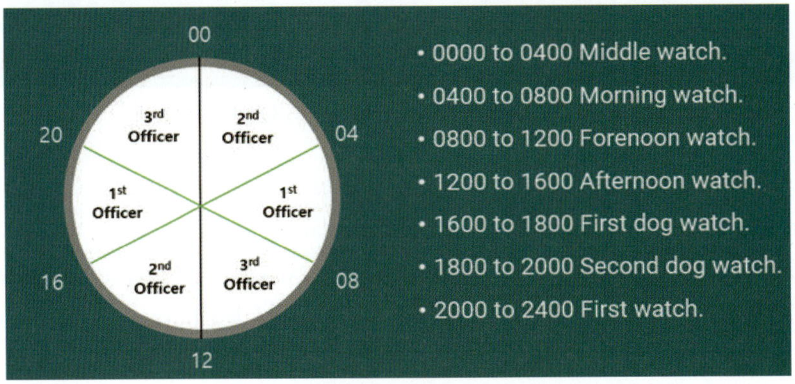

Fig. 8.3 Bridge watch schedule

8.3 Navigation Equipment

The vessel's navigation equipment consists of devices that determine the ship's position, speed, and course and ensure safety during navigation in shallow waters or when meeting other ships. Most of them have been used by seafarers for a long time, while some have been replaced with new technologies. All bridge equipment should be regularly checked and tested. The list of the minimum shipborne navigational equipment depends on the ship's tonnage, its destination and date of construction. It is defined by SOLAS Chapter V, Regulation 19.

8.3.1 Compass

A compass is a device that shows the cardinal directions used for navigation and geographic orientation. It commonly consists of a magnetized needle or other elements, such as a compass card or compass rose, which can pivot to align itself with the magnetic north. Other methods may be used, including gyroscopes, magnetometers, and GPS receivers. Compasses often show angles in degrees: north corresponds to 0°, and the angles increase clockwise, so east means 90°, south is 180°, and west is 270°. These numbers allow the compass to show azimuths or bearings, which are commonly stated in degrees. If the local variation between magnetic north and true north is known, then the direction of magnetic north also gives the direction of true north.

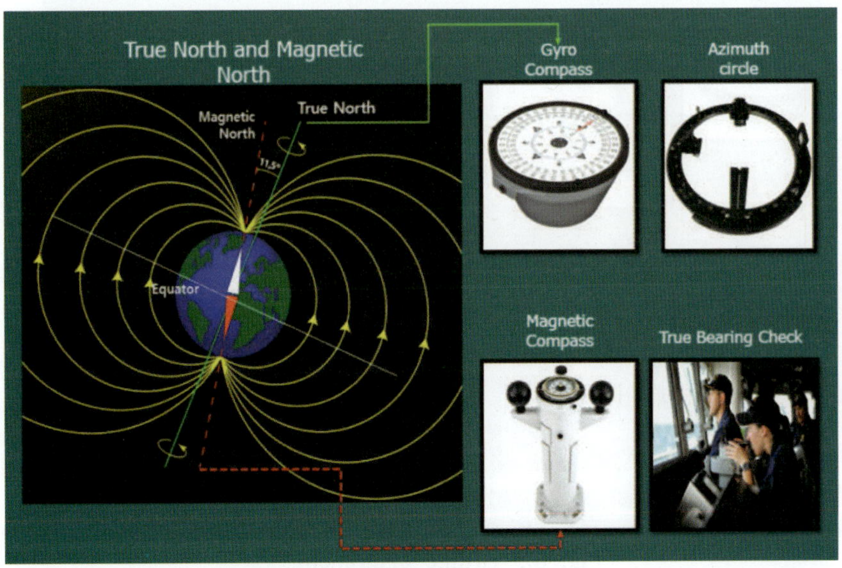

Fig. 8.4 Compass and bearing

Table 8.1 Terms of compass and bearing

Term	Meaning
Magnetic north	Magnetic north is the direction that a compass needle points to as it aligns with the Earth's magnetic field.
True north	True north is the direction that points directly towards the geographic North Pole. This is a fixed point on the Earth's globe.
Azimuth	The horizontal direction in degrees of a celestial point from a terrestrial point.
Bearing	The horizontal angle at a given point measured clockwise from a specific datum to a second point.

8.3.2 Bridge equipment

A navigation officer uses various types of electronic bridge equipment for the ship's navigation. The primary purpose is to know the position, speed, heading, time requirements for arriving at the destination, communication, signalling, avoiding collision and accident, distress management, etc. The following figure depicts an overview of navigation equipment fitted on the bridge.

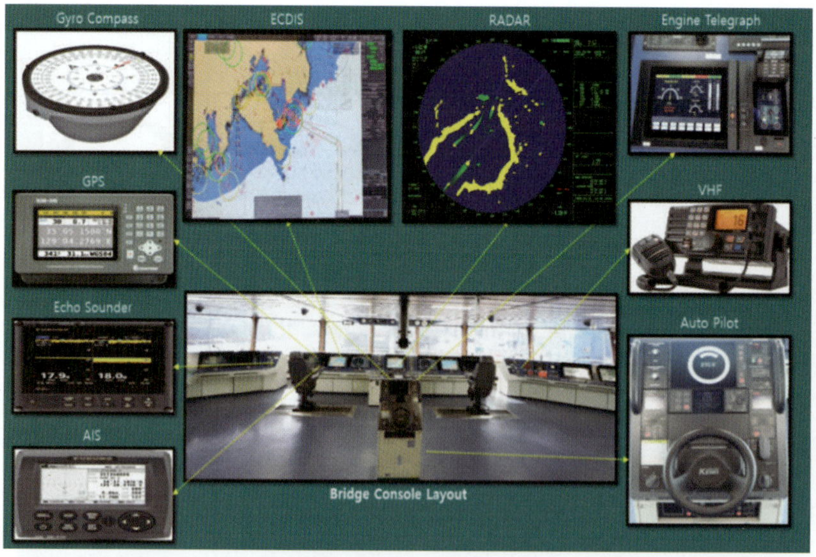

Fig. 8.5 Bridge equipment

Table 8.2 Bridge equipment

Term	Meaning
Gyro compass	A true north-seeking gyroscope fitted with a compass card and housing.
GPS	**Global Positioning System** A satellite - based navigation system operated and maintained by the US Department of Defense. GPS consists of a constellation of 24 satellites providing worldwide, 24 - hour, three dimensional (3D) coverage. Although originally conceived for military needs, GPS has a broad array of civilian applications including survey, marine, land, aviation, and vehicular navigation.
AIS	**Automatic Identification System** A novel radar-based system displaying ship's unique identification numbers alongside the radar vectors. AIS equipment consists of a central unit that collates information from the ship's navigation systems with preprogrammed information about the ship's identity and dimensions and additional information such as voyage details. The information is transmitted automatically to other ships and coastal VTS by way of transponder operating in the VHF marine band.
Echo sounder	An instrument in which a pulse of energy is converted to sound energy and transmitted downward by means of a transducer on a vessel's hull. When the energy strikes the bottom or an object with density different from the ambient water, it returns as an echo to the transducer to be reconverted to electrical energy to indicate either the depth of the water or the depth of the obeject.
ECDIS	**Electronic Chart Display and Information System** The newly developed navigational tool using digital charts (vectorised and raster charts) for navigational tasks normally carried out with paper charts. The equipment must be type - approved and uses up-to-date official charts. As long as the area covered by vector charts (ENC) is small, the ECDIS should be able to cover both vector and raster (RNC) charts. When operating in raster mode, an ECDIS must be used together with an appropriate folio of up-to-date paper charts.

RADAR	**RAdio Detection And Ranging** An electronic navigation aid using radio waves sent out as a narrow beam to detect solid objects around the ship. Any solid object of a reasonable size reflects the beam and is detected on the radar screen as a bright spot. Two systems are usually required for larger ships, one main S-band and one auxiliary X-band. A system consists of a transmitter-modulator, receiver, a rotatable directional antenna (scanner), required power supplies, a master indicator, and remote indicators (when desired).
VHF	**Very High Frequency** The direct method of voice communication. It is limited in range with normal equipment to under 100 miles, though this distance will vary according to weather and atmospheric conditions.
Auto Pilot	Automatic control system used for automatic navigation. The system can sense the difference between the ordered course of the ship and the actual course and will cause the rudder to move to an angle proportional to this error. The autopilot keeps the vessel on the correct heading without the helmsman's intervention.

8.4 Radio Equipment

Marine communication between ships or with the shore was carried out with the help of onboard systems through shore stations and even satellites. While ship-to-ship communication was brought about by VHF radio, Digital Selective Calling (DSC) came up with digitally remote control commands to transmit or receive distress alerts, urgent or safety calls, or routine priority messages. DSC controllers can now be integrated with the VHF radio as per the SOLAS (Safety Of Life at Sea) convention.

8.4.1 GMDSS

Global Maritime Distress and Safety System (GMDSS) uses Earth and satellite technologies and ship radio systems. The components of this system on the ship are VHF, MF/HF with DSC, Navtex, radio telex, SART, EPIRB, and Inmarsat - C.

The GMDSS console is used to notify the coastal services of emergencies with vessels and receive maritime safety messages, and communicate with other ships by radio.

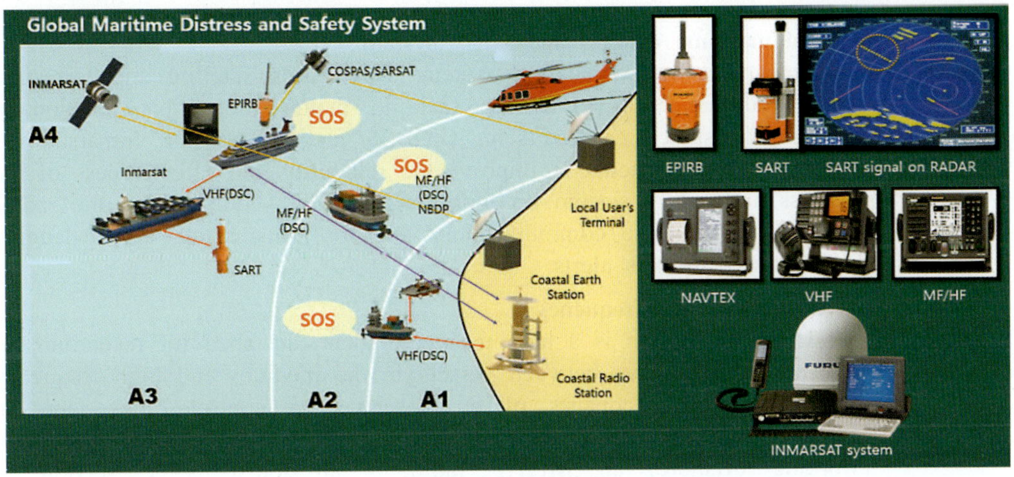

Fig. 8.6 GMDSS

Under international requirements, the GMDSS defines four sea areas: A1, A2, A3 and A4. Such division allows tracking areas where GMDSS services are available and defining what radio equipment ships must carry (as the type of radio safety equipment depends upon the GMDSS areas in which ships travel).

- A1 – 20 - 30 nautical miles from coast station – at least one VHF coast station covers this area. The continuous digital selective calling (Ch.70 / 156.525 MHz) alerting and radiotelephony services are available.
- A2 – the area within the coverage of at least one coast MF radio station providing continuous monitoring at a frequency of 2187.5 kHz (DSC) and radio communications in telephony mode at 2182 kHz (100 - 150 nautical miles), except for the area A1.

- A3 – the area within the zone of coverage of geostationary satellites I NMARSAT (approximately 70 °N and 70 °S) with the exception of a reas A1 and A2.
- A4 – this area is beyond all other ones. It includes the Polar Regions, North and South of about 76 degrees of latitude.

Table 8.3 Terms of GMDSS

Term	Meaning
GMDSS	**Global maritime distress and safety system** An integrated communication system which uses satellite and terrestrial radio communication to ensure that no matter the ship's position in distress, assistance can be sent. GMDSS incorporates the Inmarsat and EPIRB satellite systems to improve the reliability and effectiveness of the distress and safety system on global basis. DSC - equipped marine radios are used for routine communications and for transmitting, acknowledging and relaying distress alerts.
MF/HF	**Medium and high frequency** MF/HF radio station is a high tech equipment, designed for receiving and transmitting messages between vessels in the medium and high frequency range. It usually consists of a transceiver, a control block, and an antenna. For any vessel crossing oceans and seas as well as for those working offshore, an MF/HF radio is an indispensable section of equipment, it ensures long-distance radio communication.
NAVTEX	An international maritime radio telex system sponsored by **IMO** and **IHO**, which automatically receives the broadcast telex information such as navigational, meteorological warnings and search and rescue (SAR) alerts on 24 - hour watch basis.
INMARSAT	**International maritime satellite** Inmarsat system is the aggregate of standards and systems (subsystems) using the same satellites and, as a rule, common Land Earth Stations, however satellite terminals differ significantly by their functions, structure and technical parameters. The main purpose of Inmarsat is to provide marine vessels with reliable communications, primarily for enhancement of shipping safety, which included transmission of SOS signals, operative interaction with other vessels and shore services, communication between crew members and passengers with the shore, and is to ensure functioning of maritime satellite communication system in accordance with the requirements of GMDSS.

COSPAS/ SARSAT	**Cosmicheskaya sistema poiska avariynyh sudov / Space system for the search of vessels in distress** COSPAS - SARSAT is a satellite-based monitoring system that detects and locates emergency beacons. Professional operators then notify search - and - rescue (SAR) authorities. The beacons comply with internationally agreed standards for radio communication and identification of beacon owners.
EPIRB	**Emergency position indicating radio beacon** The 406 MHz satellite EPIRB is a small battery - powered transmitting device designed to provide rapid alerting, identification and accurate location information to search and rescue crews. As the name implies, it is used only in case of emergency and usually only as a last resort when your marine radio is inoperable or out of range.
SART	**Search and rescue radar transponder** A portable transmitter designed for survivor location during search and rescue operations. Fitting a SART enables a survival craft to show up on a search vessel radar display as an easily recognized series of dots.
DSC	**Digital selective calling** A technique using digital codes. It enables a radio station to establish contact with, and transfer information to, other stations complying with the relevant recommendations of the International Radio Consultative Committee (CCIR).

8.5 Meteorology

8.5.1 Wind

The Beaufort scale is an empirical measure that relates wind speed to observed conditions at sea or on land. Internationally, WMO Manual on Marine Meteorological Services (2012 edition) defined the Beaufort Scale as only up to force 12, and there was no recommendation on the use of the extended scale.

Table 8.4 Beaufort scale

Scale	Wind speed
0	Calm (< 1 knot)
1	Light air (1 - 3 knot)
2	Light breeze (4 - 6 knot)
3	Gentle breeze (7 - 10 knot)
4	Moderate breeze (11 - 16 knot)
5	Fresh breeze (17 - 21 knot)
6	Strong breeze (22 - 27 knot)
7	Moderate gale (28 - 33 knot)
8	Fresh gale (34 - 40 knot)
9	Strong gale (41 - 47 knot)
10	Storm (48 - 55 knot)
11	Violent storm (56 - 63 knot)
12	Hurricane (> 64 knot)

Wind direction is generally reported by the direction from which it originates. For example, a south - east wind blows from the south - east to the north - west.

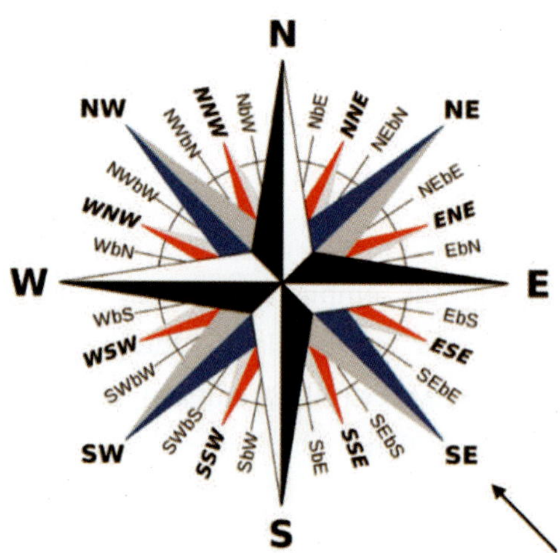

Fig. 8.7 Wind direction

A tropical storm is a rapidly rotating storm system characterized by a low - pressure center, a closed low - level atmospheric circulation, strong winds, and a spiral arrangement of thunderstorms that produce heavy rain and/or squalls. Depending on its location and strength, a tropical cyclone is referred to by different names, including **hurricane, typhoon, and cyclone.**

Fig. 8.8 Tropical storms

8.5.2 Sea state

In oceanography, the sea state is the general condition of the free surface on a large body of water concerning wind waves and swell at a certain location and moment. A sea state is characterized by statistics, including the wave height, period, and spectrum. The sea state varies with time as the wind or swell conditions change. An experienced observer can assess the sea state, like a trained mariner or through instruments like weather buoys, wave radar, or remote sensing satellites.

The World Meteorological Organization (WMO) sea state code largely adopts the 'wind sea' definition of the Douglas Sea Scale as below.

Table 8.5 Scale for sea state

Scale		Height of waves
0	Calm (glassy)	0.0 meters
1	Calm (rippled)	0.0 – 0.1 m
2	Smooth (wavelets)	0.1 – 0.5 m
3	Slight	0.5 – 1.25 m
4	Moderate	1.25 – 2.50 m
5	Rough	2.50 – 4.00 m
6	Very rough	4.00 – 6.00 m
7	High	6.00 – 9.00 m
8	Very high	9.00 – 14.00 m
9	Phenomenal	> 14.00 m

8.5.3 Tide

Tides are the rise and fall of sea levels caused by the combined effects of the gravitational forces exerted by the Moon and the Sun and the rotation of the Earth.

Tide changes proceed via the two main stages:

- The water stops falling, reaching a local minimum called low tide.
- The water stops rising, reaching a local maximum called high tide.

In some regions, there are additional two possible stages:

- Sea level rises over several hours, covering the intertidal zone; flood tide.
- The sea level falls over several hours, revealing the intertidal zone; ebb tide.

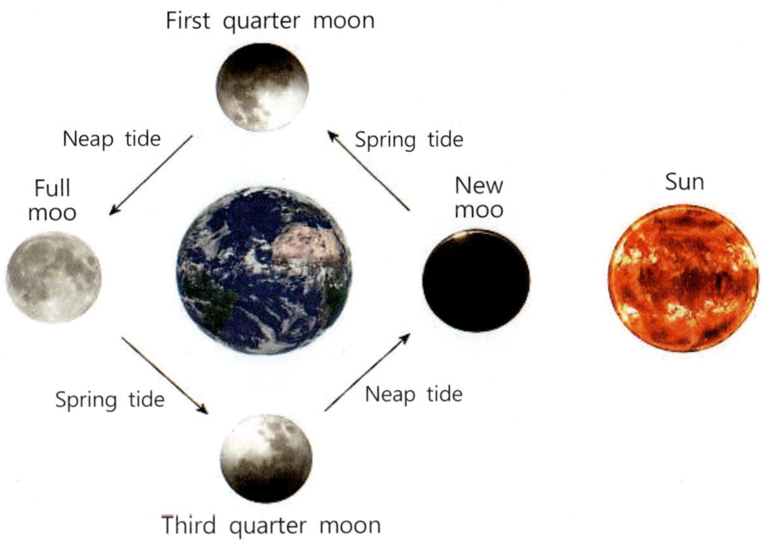

Fig. 8.9 Tide schemetic

The semi - diurnal range (the difference in height between high and low waters over about half a day) varies in a two - week cycle. Approximately twice a month, around the new Moon and full Moon, when the Sun, Moon, and Earth form a line, the tidal force due to the Sun reinforces that due to the Moon. The tide's range is then at its maximum; this is called the spring tide. When the Moon is in the first quarter or third quarter, the Sun and Moon are separated by 90° when viewed from the Earth, and the solar, tidal force partially cancels the Moon's tidal force. At these points in the lunar cycle, the tide's range is at its minimum; this is called the neap tide. Oscillating currents produced by tides are known as tidal streams or tidal currents. The moment that the tidal current ceases is called slack water or slack tide. The tide then reverses direction and is said to be turning. Slack water usually occurs near high water and low water, but there are locations where the moments of slack tide differ significantly from those of high and low water.

The following reference tide levels can be defined, from the highest level to the lowest:

- Highest astronomical tide (HAT) – The highest tide can be predicted to occur. Note that meteorological conditions may add extra height to the HAT.
- Mean high water springs (MHWS) – The average of the two high tides on the days of spring tides.
- Mean high water neaps (MHWN) – The average of the two high tides on the days of neap tides.
- Mean sea level (MSL) – This is the average sea level. The MSL is constant for any location over a long period.
- Mean low water neaps (MLWN) – The average of the two low tides on the days of neap tides.
- Mean low water springs (MLWS) – The average of the two low tides on the days of spring tides.
- Lowest astronomical tide (LAT) – The lowest tide which can be predicted to occur

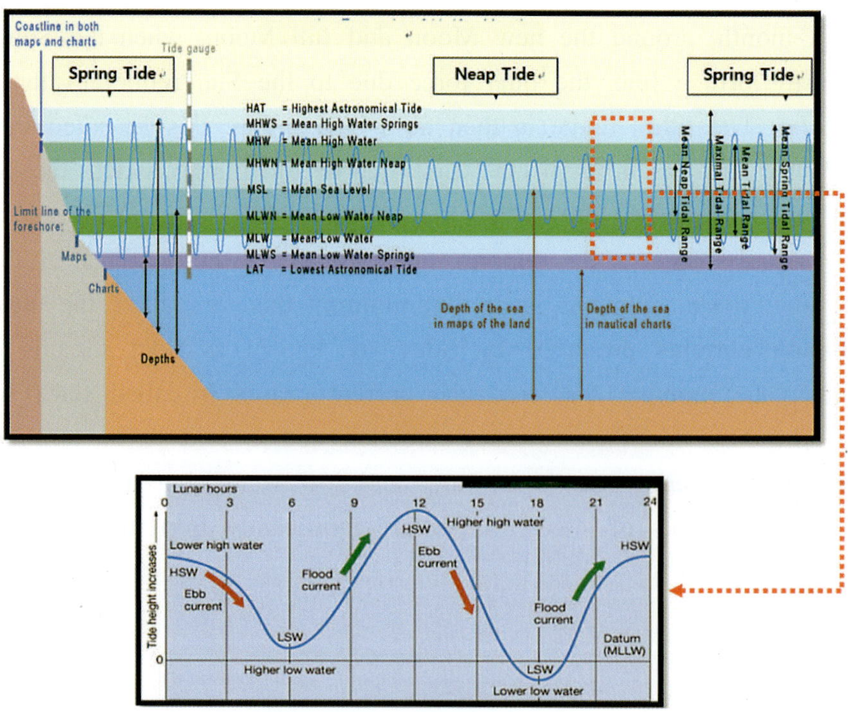

Fig. 8.10 Tidal oscillation

8.5.4 Fog and visibility scale

Marine fog commonly occurs worldwide due to the various physical, chemical, dynamical, and radiative processes active at various time and space scales.

Marine fog impacts transportation and shipping, aviation, and the Earth ecosystem because of reduced visibilities and increased moisture availability.

Table 8.6 Scale for fog

Scale		Status in N. M
0	Dense fog	Less than 45 meters
1	Thick fog	Less than 180 meters
2	Fog	Less than 360 meters
3	Moderate fog	Less than 0.5 N.M.
4	Thin fog	Less than 1 N.M.
5	Poor visibility	Less than 2 N.M.
6	Moderate visibility	Less than 5 N.M.
7	Good visibility	Less than 10 N.M.
8	Very good visibility	Less than 30 N.M.
9	Excellent visibility	More than 30 N.M.

A foghorn or fog signal is a device that uses sound to warn vehicles of navigational hazards such as rocky coastlines, or the presence of other ships, in foggy conditions. All vessels, whether stationary or moving, are required by law to utilize fog signals in inclement weather; the type, number, length, and timing of the signal indicate the size of the vessel and its position. The nature and application of fog warnings are codified in the International Regulations for Preventing Collisions at Sea (commonly called International Rules of the Road), applicable to all international waters.

8.6 Engine Room Duty, Patrol, Deadman Alarm

8.6.1 Engine room duty & Patrol

The ship's engine room work can be divided into daily and watch - keeping work systems.

UMS refers to the unattended machine space system specified by the classification. During a regular voyage, it is possible to remotely control the engine from the bridge without a duty engineer in the machinery space and monitor various equipment running status in the engine room. In addition, various alarm systems are activated to be recognized from the bridge and interior areas.

There are different terminologies used by classification societies as follows.

- ABS : ACCU (Automatic Control System Certified for Unattended engine room)
- LR : UMS (Unattended Machinery Space)
- NK : M.O (Man ZerO)
- KR : UMA (Unattended Machinery Area)
- DNV : E.O (Engine room ZerO)

Fig. 8.11 Engine Control Room

Daily work means that all seafarers in the engine room perform their duties during the daytime and maintain the engine room in an unmanned state outside of regular hours. In this way of working, seafarers of the engine department work from 09:00 to 18:00, and the seafarers do not work in the engine room from 18:00 to 09:00 the next day. At this time, only the duty engineer responds by using the Alarm Monitoring System(AMS) in their bedroom. In the on - call duty, it is carried out in special situations such as arrival/departure from a port, during unloading work and passing through a narrow waterway. The working hours for each engineer are set.

The first engineer works from 04:00 to 08:00, 16:00 to 20:00, the second engineer from 00:00 to 04:00, 12:00 to 16:00, and the third engineer from 08 to 12:00 and 20:00 to 24:00.

Most of the recently built ships maintain the unmanned watch system, and the procedure for change of watch in the case of an unmanned watch is as follows (*There may be differences depending on the ship).

The duty engineer must prepare the engine room checklist, check the equipment leakage, transfer the bilge and sludge and carry out the cleaning work. In the case of converting the engine room to an unmanned watch, contact the bridge, change the duty call and record it in the engine room logbook.

During the night patrol of the engine room, the engineer on duty contacts the bridge, activate the Deadman alarm system, enters the engine room, and changes the engine room to attend. Patrol records according to UMA Checklist. After completing the patrol, contact the bridge before leaving the engine room and change to duty call before leaving the engine room. Turn off Deadman Alarm after leaving the engine room. After entering the engine room the following day, contact the bridge, change the engine room to attend and fill in the engine room logbook.

DATE OF INSPECTION				MM/DD											
RANK OF DUTY ENGINEER				SIGN											
CHIEF ENGINEER				SIGN											
M/T TELEGRAPH															
M/T RPM INDICATOR															
SHIP SPEED INDICATOR															
REV. COUNTER															
M/T SUB CONT. PANEL	LAMP TEST			OK											
	MAIN COND. VACUUM			mmHg											
	M/T INLET STEAM PRES.			kg/cm2											
	MANUE. V/V LIFT / RPM			mm / rpm											
	HPT STEAM CHEST PRESS.			kg/cm2											
	HPT 1ST STAGE STM PRESS.			kg/cm2											
	M/T LUB. OIL INLET PRESS.			kg/cm2											
	M/T LEVER POS. INDICATOR			W.E											
DISPLAY UNIT FOR SPM	SHAFT SPEED			RPM											
	SHAFT POWER			BHP											
	SHAFT TOTAL REVOLUTION			RPM											
VIBRATION	MAIN TURBINE	VIB	HPT	μm											
			LPT	μm											
			R/G (HP/LP)	mm/sec											
		POS	HPT	mm											
			LPT	mm											
			MAIN THRUST	mm											
NO.1 L.O STOR TANK LEVEL				TON											
NO.2 L.O STOR TANK LEVEL				TON											

Fig. 8.12 UMS Checklist

Deadman alarm system (* Deadman alarm application time may vary depending on a ship)

The reset button installed in the engine room should be pressed periodically during the engine room patrol. It is used to check the safety of the watch engine room in evening patrol. The installation location is at the engine room entrance and the engine control room. Reset is possible at various places in the engine room during patrol.

If reset is not done within 3 minutes, a pre - warning alarm in the engine room and engineer's bedroom on the watch occurs. If reset action is not done within 27 minutes, an alarm will activates sound in all engineer's bedrooms, living quarters, and bridge to respond.

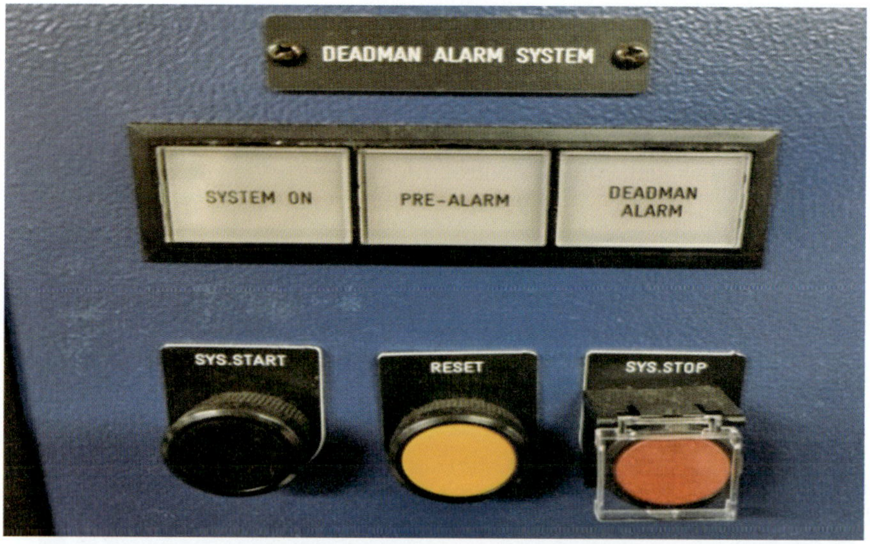

Fig. 8.13 Deadman alarm system

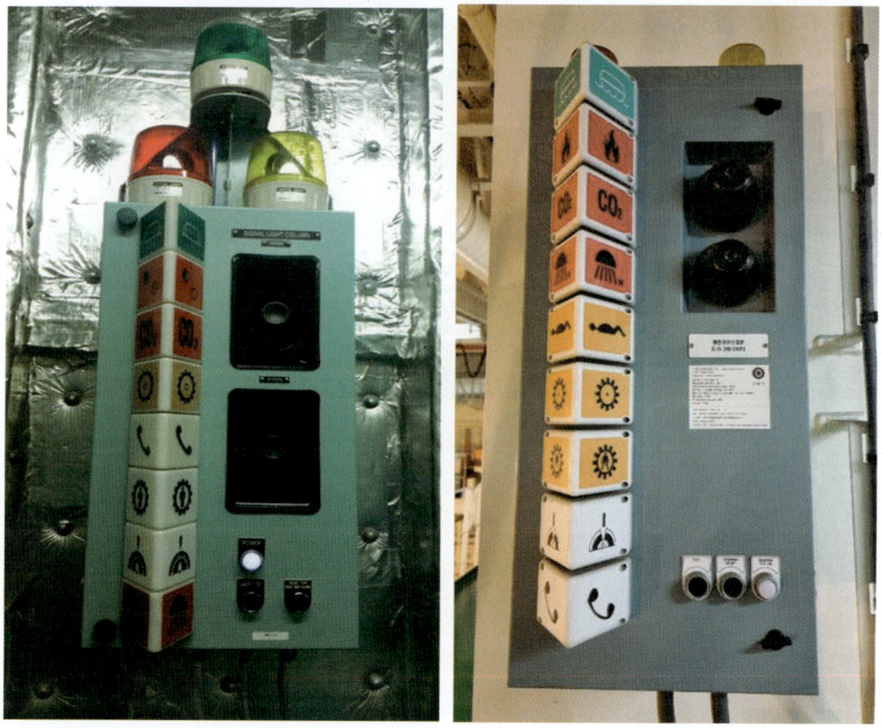

Fig. 8.14 Deadman alarm system reset button in engine room

Engineer's call

It refers to a system that can call the designated engineer when communication is not smooth due to poor communication on board or other reasons. It can be called from Bridge and engine control room.

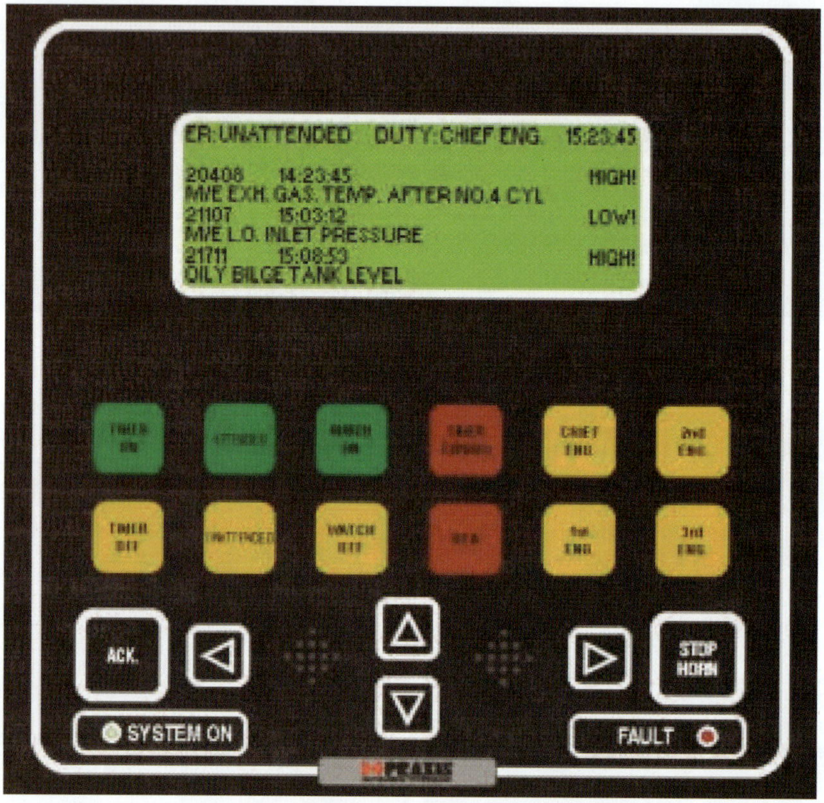

Fig. 8.15 Engineer's call

Exercise

Chapter.8

1. Write down key words in this chapter

2. Summarize the content in this chapter.

✓ **Speed Quiz** – Explain the meaning of the word and Answer the word

Practice

1. Image the word

2. Make the sentence

3. Make your team and story

4. Set the role

5. Presentation with video recording

6. Self-evaluation

7. Feedback

Presentation Evaluation sheet

Team Presenter

Title

1. Topic clear

1	2	3	4	5	6	7	8	9	10

2. Voice clearance

1	2	3	4	5	6	7	8	9	10

3. Presentation Material

1	2	3	4	5	6	7	8	9	10

4. Maritime Word

1	2	3	4	5	6	7	8	9	10

5. Grammar

1	2	3	4	5	6	7	8	9	10

6. Expression (Body language)

1	2	3	4	5	6	7	8	9	10

7. pace

1	2	3	4	5	6	7	8	9	10

8. story structure

1	2	3	4	5	6	7	8	9	10

9. Q & A

1	2	3	4	5	6	7	8	9	10

10. Overall score

1	2	3	4	5	6	7	8	9	10

✓ **Feedback opinion**

Date ____________ Evaluator ____________

9

Fire and Life Saving Equipment

9.1 Fire-Fighting Appliances

9.2 Personal Life-Saving Appliances

9.3 Drill

9.1 Fire - Fighting Appliances

In the modern shipping industry, one of the main causes of accidents onboard ships is fire. This is because of high temperature, the excess quantity of flammable oil and other combustible materials. A ship is approved to sail in international waters only if constructed as per the Fire Safety System Code (FSS Code) and carries required Fire Fighting Appliances approved by the concerned authority. A ship is fitted with various types of fire retardant and fire - fighting equipment to fight any fire and extinguish it as soon as possible before it turns into a major catastrophic situation. Fire protection on ships is provided by detection and fire - fighting equipment together with structural features which are intended to contain an outbreak of fire and the employment when required of non - combustible materials to prevent its spread. This section will explain a list of crucial fire-fighting equipment and measures present on board.

9.1.1 Fire - fighters' outfit

A fireman's outfit is used onboard ships, which are donned by the fire - fighter designated crew to fight the fire.

Fig. 9.1 Fire fighting outfit

Fig. 9.2 Fire fighting outfit

9.1.2 Emergency Escape Breathing Devices (EEBD)

EEBDs are self-contained compressed air apparatuses which supply the seafarers with breathable oxygen to help them safely escape from contamination areas on a ship.

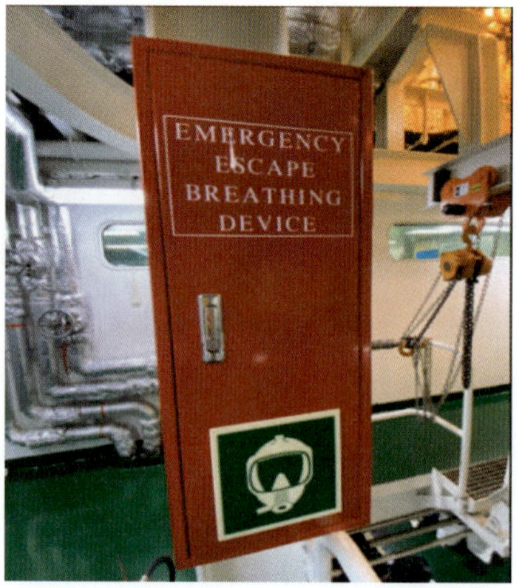

Fig. 9.3 Emergency escape breathing device

Fig. 9.4 Emergency escape breathing device

9.1.3 Fire extinguisher

When there is a fire, all attempts are to be made to get it extinguished. There are various means of fire - fighting, with different objectives: take away heat, oxygen or the flammable material to prevent combustion.

Fig. 9.5 Fire extinguishers

Table 9.1 Overview of fire classes

Class	Type of fules	Detailed goods
A	Solids	Wood, paper, textile, plastics
B	Liquids	Liquifying goods, petrol, alcohol, sterane, fat, tar, paint
C	Cases	LPG, butane, propane
D	Metals	Magnesium, aluminium, titanium, zirkonium, sodium, potassium

(1) Portable fire extinguisher

The first line of defence onboard usually is the portable fire - extinguisher such as Dry - powder, CO_2 or foam.

- **Dry - powder**
  This extinguisher contains sodium bicarbonate powder with a waterproofing agent such as magnesium stearate to prevent caking.

Fig. 9.6 Dry powder fire extinguisher

- **CO_2 Fire extinguisher**

  The soda - acid extinguisher has largely been replaced by the CO_2/ water type, which does not rely on chemical action for its operation.

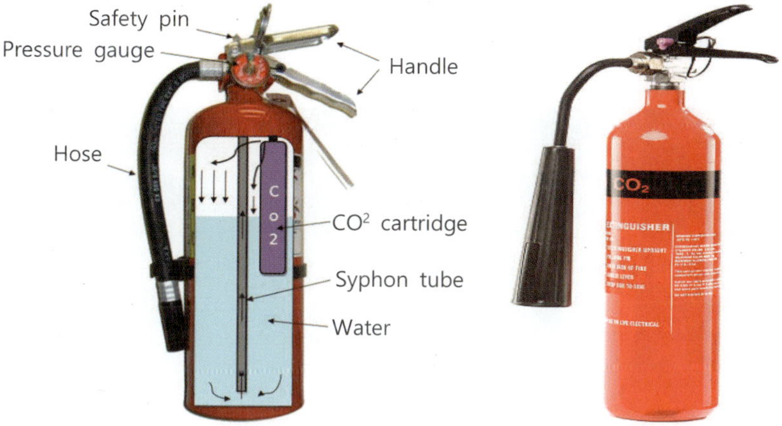

Fig. 9.7 Co_2 Fire extinguisher

- **Foam fire extinguisher**

  The outer casing of the portable (chemical) foam extinguisher is similar in construction to the soda-acid appliance and is required to withstand the same initial test pressure of 25 bar and is retested at 21 bar every four years.

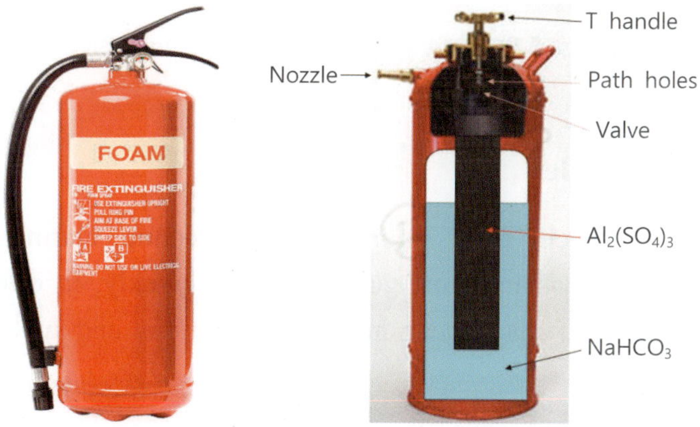

Fig. 9.8 Foam fire extinguisher

9.1.4 Fixed gas fire - extinguishing systems

Fix gas fire - system is filling a space with a gas which reduces the oxygen content, or which is an anticatalyst. It reduces the oxygen content to a level where fire cannot exist. Fixed gas fire - extinguishing systems uses in engine rooms and cargo hold to fight the fire.

Fig. 9.9 Fixed Co_2 fire extinguishing system

9.1.5 Automatic sprinkler

The sprinkler system is an automatic fire detecting, alarm and extinguishing system which is constantly on guard to deal quickly & effectively with the outbreak of fire that may occur in accommodations and other spaces.

Fig. 9.10 Sprinkler

9.1.6 Fixed fire detection and fire alarm systems

(1) Fire detection

Fire detectors are designed to provide a visible and audible alarm on the vessel to indicate the location of a fire.

- **Flame detectors**

  A flame detector is an optical sensory device designed to detect flames.

Fig. 9.11 Flame fire detector

- **Heat detectors**

A heat detector is a fire alarm device designed to respond when the converted thermal energy of a fire increases the temperature of a heat-sensitive element.

Fig. 9.12 Heat fire detector

- **Smoke detectors**

A smoke detector is a device that senses smoke, typically as an indicator of fire.

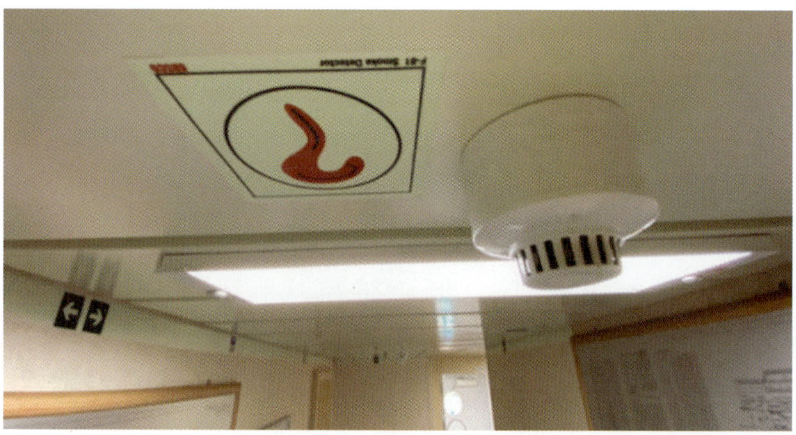

Fig. 9.13 Smoke fire detector

(2) Fire alarm system

The fire alarm, a bell that rings loudly at intervals of a few seconds, can be activated manually by pushing a button in a red box behind glass. The alarm buttons are installed throughout the ship. The alarm reset can only be done at the main display, usually on the bridge. On display can be seen which button, in which zone of detection - loop, is activated. A zone of the loop (i.e., engine room) can be isolated when repairs are carried out, and smoke at that location is inevitable.

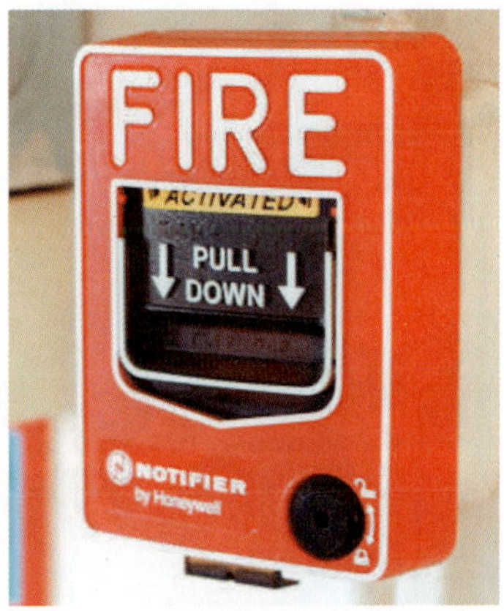

Fig. 9.14 Fire alarm

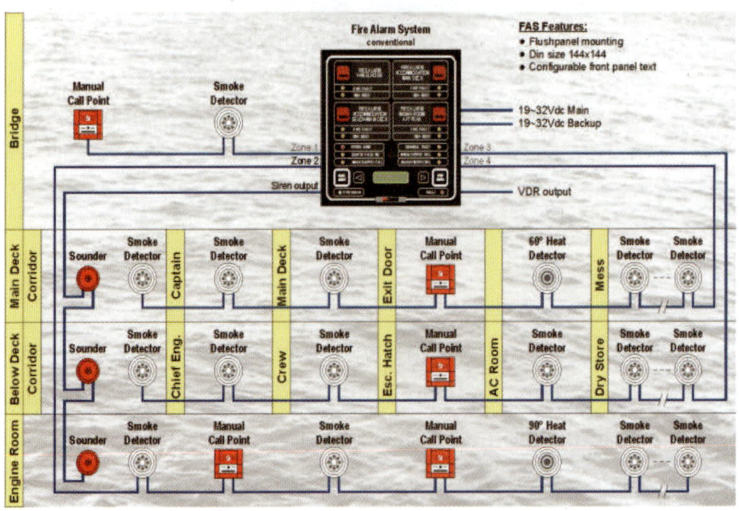

Fig. 9.15 Fire alarm system

9.1.7 Emergency fire pump

It is a fixed emergency fire pump independently driven by a self-cooled compression ignition engine or an electric motor whose power is supplied from an emergency generator. Emergency fire pumps can still be used when they are out of action, either by disabling the pumps or their power source.

Fig. 9.16 Emergency fire pump

9.2 Personal Life-Saving Appliances

9.2.1 Lifebuoys

A lifebuoy is a life-saving buoy designed to be thrown to a person in the water to provide buoyancy and prevent drowning. They comprise many buoys attached to the handrails, some with a floating line, some with a floating light. On both bridge wings, there has to be a lifebuoy. Attached to these buoys are a floating smoke light and a light signal.

Fig. 9.17 Life buoy

9.2.2 Life jackets

A life jacket is a sleeveless jacket made up of buoyant or inflatable material used to keep the human body afloat in water. Life jackets are essential safety equipment on ships as personal life - saving appliances. There are mostly stored in the cabins and in the lifeboats' boxes. They have to be provided with reflective materials. A whistle and a light have to be attached.

Fig. 9.18 Life jacket

9.2.3 Immersion suits

An immersion suit is a body covering suit that is worn specifically to remain afloat and survive during emergencies. Immersion suits are designed to prevent crews from death due to exposure and hypothermia. Hypothermia is the most dangerous threat to people. The insulating quality of immersion suits has to be such that the body temperature has not dropped more than two after six hours in water with a temperature between 0℃ and 2℃.

Fig. 9.19 Immersion suits

9.2.4 Survival craft

(1) Life rafts

Life Rafts are provided as a life - saving appliance on every seagoing merchant or passenger ship, in addition to the life boats. Inflatable Life Rafts are available on each side for the whole complement. They are to be dropped overboard, where an attached line arranges the inflation. In case the ship sinks, a hydrostatic release releases the raft.

Fig. 9.20 Life raft

Fig. 9.21 Life raft

(2) Lifeboats

A lifeboat is a small, rigid or inflatable boat carried for emergency evacuation in the event of a disaster aboard a ship. Lifeboats on each side of the ship, capable of accommodating everybody on board on each side, or one free-fall life at the poop with capacity for the whole complement are the essential items. The capacity of the lifeboats depends on the number of people carried on board. Every lifeboat must have a diesel engine, starting with batteries and backed up by a manual starting system. Lifeboat installations that use gravity as an energy source are usually of the 'free fall' type.

Fig. 9.22 Lifeboats

Fig. 9.23 Lifeboat

(3) Rescue Boats

A rescue boat is a boat rescue craft which is used to attend to a ship in distress, or its survivors, to rescue crew and passengers. It can be hand-pulled, sail-powered or powered by an engine.

Fig. 9.24 Rescue boat

9.3 Drill

Drills are methods of practicing how a team or individuals should behave in an emergency on board a ship. To respond an accident quickly, people need to be trained. Regular drills, fire - fighting drills, and abandon - ship drills have to be carried out and are compulsory. The drills must be as realistic as possible. On completion of the drill, an evaluation has to be made, where the shortcomings of the group or the individuals are to be discussed, and, if necessary, some theory is reviewed. The drills must be recorded in the ships' logbooks.

Table 9.2 Lists of ships' drill

Drills	Goal	How many times ?
Abandon ship	The drills are aimed to prepare all crews for any emergency evacuation that may take place in the event of a fire or call to abandon ship.	Every month
Fire – fighting	A fire drill is a method of practicing how to they are extinguishing fire onboard and handling fire-fighting appliances.	Every month
Emergency steering	An emergency steering drill should be carried out every month in the steering gear room with proper communication with a bridge to train all the ship's staff for proper operation of the system so that in an emergency, ship control can be regained as soon as possible, avoiding collision or grounding.	Once every three months

Fig. 9.25 Abandon ship drill

Fig. 9.26 Abandon ship drill

9.3.1 Muster list

A muster list for crews to look at, with their names and functions and the particular tasks during fire or emergencies, is fitted on the walls at various places; each cabin, wheelhouse, mess rooms, fire - control station, etc.

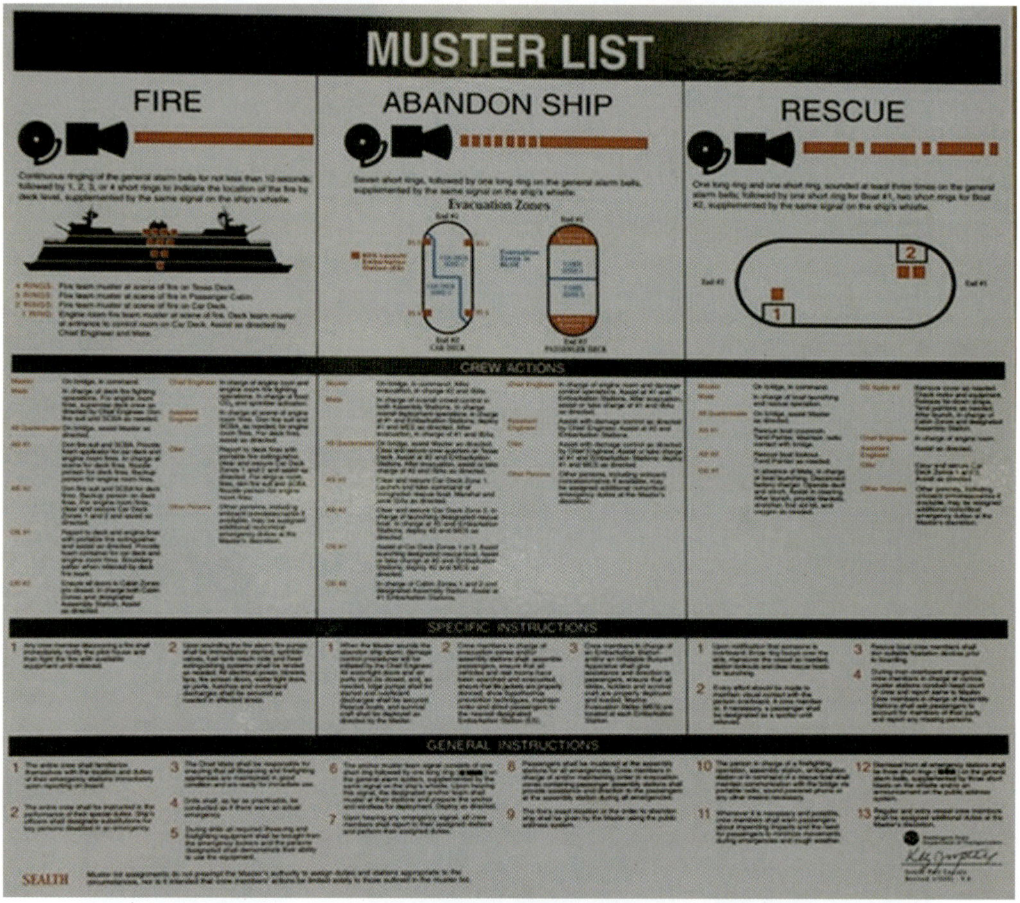

Fig. 9.27 Muster List

Exercise

Chapter.9

1. Write down key words in this chapter

2. Summarize the content in this chapter.

✍ Practice Ⅰ

1. Image the word

2. Make the sentence

3. Make your team and story

4. Set the role

5. Presentation with video recording

6. Self-evaluation

7. Feedback

Presentation Evaluation sheet

Team Presenter

Title

1. Topic clear

1	2	3	4	5	6	7	8	9	10

2. Voice clearance

1	2	3	4	5	6	7	8	9	10

3. Presentation Material

1	2	3	4	5	6	7	8	9	10

4. Maritime Word

1	2	3	4	5	6	7	8	9	10

5. Grammar

1	2	3	4	5	6	7	8	9	10

6. Expression (Body language)

1	2	3	4	5	6	7	8	9	10

7. pace

1	2	3	4	5	6	7	8	9	10

8. story structure

1	2	3	4	5	6	7	8	9	10

9. Q & A

1	2	3	4	5	6	7	8	9	10

10. Overall score

1	2	3	4	5	6	7	8	9	10

✓ **Feedback opinion**

Date ____________

Evaluator ____________

✍ Practice Ⅱ

1. Image the word

2. Make the sentence

3. Make your team and story

4. Set the role

5. Presentation with video recording

6. Self-evaluation

7. Feedback

Presentation Evaluation sheet

Team Presenter ____

Title ____

1. Topic clear

1	2	3	4	5	6	7	8	9	10

2. Voice clearance

1	2	3	4	5	6	7	8	9	10

3. Presentation Material

1	2	3	4	5	6	7	8	9	10

4. Maritime Word

1	2	3	4	5	6	7	8	9	10

5. Grammar

1	2	3	4	5	6	7	8	9	10

6. Expression (Body language)

1	2	3	4	5	6	7	8	9	10

7. pace

1	2	3	4	5	6	7	8	9	10

8. story structure

1	2	3	4	5	6	7	8	9	10

9. Q & A

1	2	3	4	5	6	7	8	9	10

10. Overall score

1	2	3	4	5	6	7	8	9	10

✓ **Feedback opinion**

Date

Evaluator

✍ Practice Ⅲ

1. Image the word

2. Make the sentence

3. Make your team and story

4. Set the role

5. Presentation with video recording

6. Self-evaluation

7. Feedback

Presentation Evaluation sheet

Team Presenter

Title

1. Topic clear

1	2	3	4	5	6	7	8	9	10

2. Voice clearance

1	2	3	4	5	6	7	8	9	10

3. Presentation Material

1	2	3	4	5	6	7	8	9	10

4. Maritime Word

1	2	3	4	5	6	7	8	9	10

5. Grammar

1	2	3	4	5	6	7	8	9	10

6. Expression (Body language)

1	2	3	4	5	6	7	8	9	10

7. pace

1	2	3	4	5	6	7	8	9	10

8. story structure

1	2	3	4	5	6	7	8	9	10

9. Q & A

1	2	3	4	5	6	7	8	9	10

10. Overall score

1	2	3	4	5	6	7	8	9	10

✓ **Feedback opinion**

Date ______________

Evaluator ______________

✍ Practice Ⅳ

1. Image the word

2. Make the sentence

3. Make your team and story

4. Set the role

5. Presentation with video recording

6. Self-evaluation

7. Feedback

Presentation Evaluation sheet

Team Presenter

Title

1. Topic clear

1	2	3	4	5	6	7	8	9	10

2. Voice clearance

1	2	3	4	5	6	7	8	9	10

3. Presentation Material

1	2	3	4	5	6	7	8	9	10

4. Maritime Word

1	2	3	4	5	6	7	8	9	10

5. Grammar

1	2	3	4	5	6	7	8	9	10

6. Expression (Body language)

1	2	3	4	5	6	7	8	9	10

7. pace

1	2	3	4	5	6	7	8	9	10

8. story structure

1	2	3	4	5	6	7	8	9	10

9. Q & A

1	2	3	4	5	6	7	8	9	10

10. Overall score

1	2	3	4	5	6	7	8	9	10

✓ **Feedback opinion**

Date ______________

Evaluator ______________

10

Relevant International Organization

10.1 International Maritime Organization

The International Maritime Organization (IMO) is the United Nations specialized agency responsible for the safety and security of shipping and the prevention of marine and atmospheric pollution by ships. As a specialized agency of the United Nations, IMO is the global standard - setting authority for the safety, security and environmental performance of international shipping. Its primary role is to create a regulatory framework for the shipping industry that is fair and effective, universally adopted and universally implemented.

Fig. 10.1 IMO

10.1.1 Purpose and role

The IMO's primary purpose is to develop and maintain a comprehensive regulatory framework for shipping and its remit today includes maritime safety, environmental concerns, legal matters, technical cooperation, maritime security and the efficiency of shipping. IMO is governed by an assembly of members and is financially administered by a council of members elected from the assembly. The work of IMO is conducted through five committees and these are supported by technical subcommittees.

10.1.2 Structure of the IMO

The IMO is governed by the IMO Assembly and the IMO Council. Beneath the Council, there are five main Committees, including the Maritime Safety Committee, the Marine Environment Protection Committee, the Legal Committee, the Technical Co-operation Committee and the Facilitation Committee.

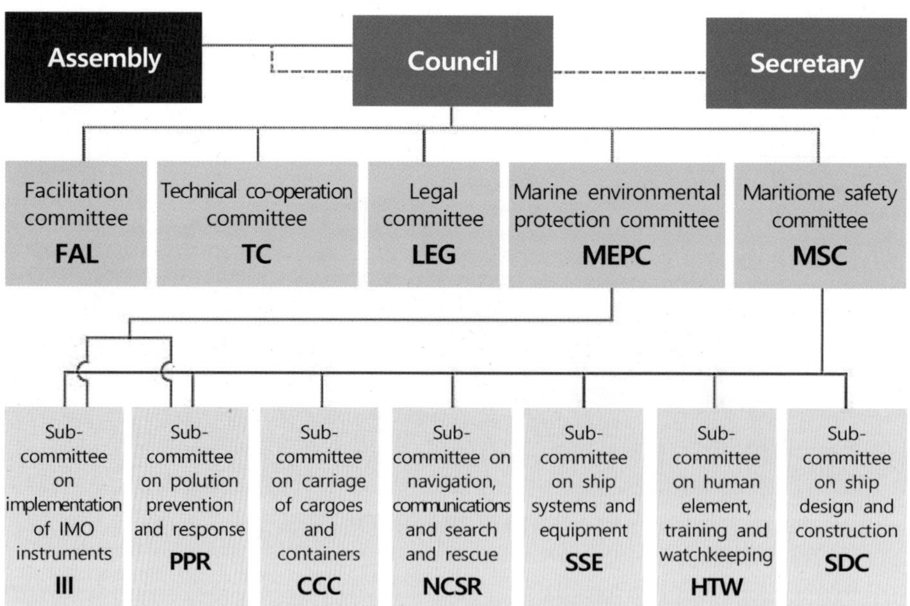

Source : https://www.classnk.or.jp/hp/en/info_service/imo_and_iacs/topics_imo.html

Fig. 10.2 Structure of IMO

Table 10.1 Committees of the IMO

Committee	Role
Maritime safety committee	The functions of the Maritime Safety Committee are to consider any matter within the scope of the Organization concerned with aids to navigation, construction and equipment of vessels, manning from a safety standpoint, rules for the prevention of collisions, handling of dangerous cargoes, maritime safety procedures and requirements, hydrographic information, log-books and navigational records, marine casualty investigations, salvage and rescue and any other matters directly affecting maritime safety.
Marine environment protection committee	The Marine Environment Protection Committee is empowered to consider any matter within the scope of the Organization concerned with prevention and control of pollution from ships.
Legal committee	The Legal Committee is empowered to deal with any legal matters within the scope of the Organization.
Technical co-operation committee	The Technical Co-operation Committee is required to consider any matter within the scope of the Organization concerned with the implementation of technical cooperation projects for which the Organization acts as the executing or cooperating agency and any other matters related to the Organization's activities in the technical cooperation field.
Facilitation committee	The Facilitation Committee deals with IMO's work in eliminating unnecessary formalities and "red tape" in international shipping by implementing all aspects of the Convention on Facilitation of International Maritime Traffic 1965 and any matter within the scope of the Organization concerned with the facilitation of international maritime traffic. In particular in recent years the Committee's work, in accordance with the wishes of the Assembly, has been to ensure that the right balance is struck between maritime security and the facilitation of international maritime trade.

10.2 International Organization Relevant to Shipping Industry

10.2.1 International labour organizaion

The International Labour Organization (ILO) is a United Nations agency whose mandate is to advance social and economic justice through setting international labour standards. Founded in October 1919 under the League of Nations, it is the first and oldest specialised agency of the UN. The ILO over the past few years include the adoption of the Maritime Labour Convention, 2006, and the Work in Fishing Convention. Adopted in February 2006, the ILO's Maritime Labour Convention sets the minimum standards to ensure satisfactory conditions of employment for the world's seafarers. It brings together and updates over 65 other ILO maritime labour instruments, while introducing a system of certification and inspection to enforce it.

Fig. 10.3 ILO

10.2.2 Non - governmental international organizations in shipping industry

(1) International Association of marine aids to navigation and Lighthouse Authorities(IALA)

The International Association of Marine Aids to Navigation and Lighthouse Authorities (IALA) is an intergovernmental organization founded in 1957 to collect and provide nautical expertise and advice.

Fig. 10.4 IALA

(2) Baltic and International Maritime Council (BIMCO)

The Baltic and International Maritime Council (BIMCO) is the world's largest direct - membership organisation for shipowners, charterers, shipbrokers and agents. At BIMCO, our mission is to be at the forefront of global developments in shipping, providing expert knowledge and practical advice to safeguard and add value to our members' businesses. The goal of BIMCO is to be the chosen partner trusted to provide leadership to the global shipping industry. BIMCO is a membership - based non-governmental organisation with offices in Copenhagen, Singapore, Shanghai, Athens and London.

(3) International Association of Classification Societies (IACS)

The International Association of Classification Societies (IACS) is a technically based non-governmental organization that currently consists of twelve member classification societies. The IACS is recognized as the principal technical advisor of IMO.

The purpose of a Classification Society is to provide classification and statutory services and assistance to the maritime industry and regulatory bodies as regards maritime safety and pollution prevention, based on the accumulation of maritime knowledge and technology. The objective of ship classification is to verify the structural strength and integrity of essential parts of the ship's hull and its appendages, and the reliability and function of the propulsion and steering systems, power generation and those other features and auxiliary systems which have been built into the ship in order to maintain essential services on board.

Table 10.2 Members of IACS

Classification societies	Country
American Bureau of Shipping (ABS)	USA
Bureau Veritas (BV)	France
China Classification Society (CCS)	China
Croatian register of shipping	Croatia
Det Norske Veritas (DNV) and Germanischer Lloyd (GL)	Norway/ Germany
Indian Register of Shipping	India
Korean Register (KR)	Korea
Lloyd's Register (LR)	Great Britain
Nippon Kaiji Kyokai (Class NK)	Japan
Polish Register of Shipping	Poland
Registro Italiano Navale (RINA)	Italy
Russian Maritime Register of Shipping (RS)	Russia

(4) International Transport workers' Federation (ITF)

The International Transport Workers' Federation (ITF) is a democratic global union federation of transport workers' trade unions. The International Transport Workers' Federation (ITF) is a democratic, affiliate - led federation recognized as the world's leading transport authority. The ITF represents the interests of transport workers' unions in bodies which take decisions affecting jobs, employment conditions or safety in the transport industry, such as the International Labour Organization (ILO), the International Maritime Organization (IMO) and the International Civil Aviation Organisation (ICAO).

(5) Comité Maritime International (CMI)

It is a non - governmental not-for - profit international organization established in Antwerp in 1897, the object of which is to contribute by all appropriate means and activities to the unification of maritime law in all its aspects. To this end it shall promote the establishment of national associations of maritime law and shall co - operate with other international organizations.

(6) International Chamber of Shipping (ICS)

The International Chamber of Shipping (ICS) is the global trade association for shipowners and operators, representing the world's national shipowner associations. The aim of ICS is to act as an advocate for the industry on issues of maritime affairs, shipping policy and technical matters, including ship construction, operation, safety and management, and to develop best practice in the industry. ICS is an international, independent, not - for - profit London-based trade association.

(7) International Maritime Pilots' Association (IMPA)

The International Maritime Pilots' Association (IMPA) is a non - profit that represents the international community of pilots. It uses the resources of its membership to promote effective safety outcomes in pilotage as an essential public service. It seeks to achieve its principal objective which is the promotion of professionally sound and safe pilotage.

(8) International association of dry cargo shipowners (INTERCARGO)

The International Association of Dry Cargo Shipowners (INTERCARGO) is an association that represents the interests of owners, operators and managers within the dry cargo shipping industry.

(9) International association of independent tanker owners (INTERTANKO)

The International Association of Independent Tanker Owners (INTERTANKO) is a membership association for owners of independent tankers throughout the world.

Fig. 10.5 Pilot

(10) International association of maritime universities

The International Association of Maritime Universities (IAMU) was founded by seven universities representing the five continents of the world (Representative Universities) in November, 1999, with a shared recognition of significance of maritime education and training in the rapid globalization of the international shipping arena. The International Association of Maritime Universities is the global network of leading maritime universities providing Maritime Education and Training (MET) of seafarers for the global shipping industry.

IAMU Structure

IAMU's Basic Agreement dictates all of IAMU's activities and the administrative structure. IAMU structure consists of an Annual General Assembly, an International Executive Board, Standing Committees, and the Secretariat.

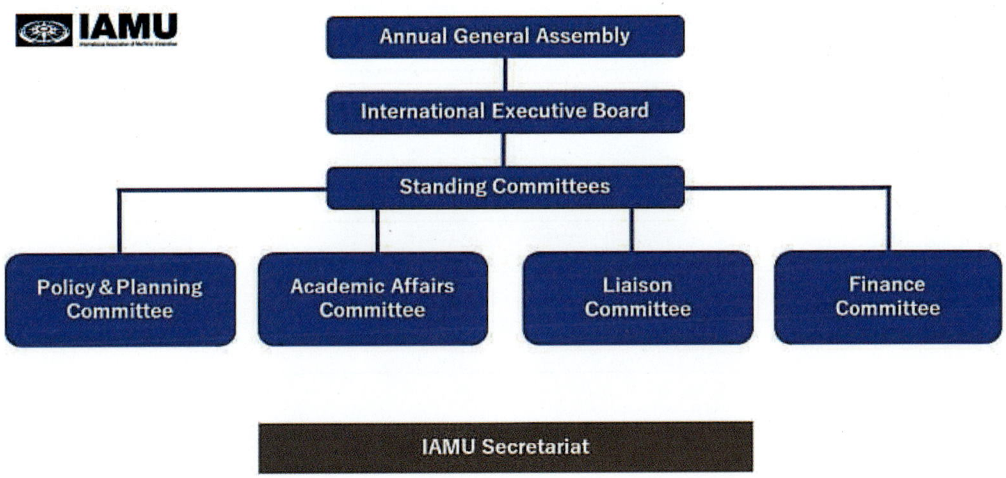

Source :https://iamu-edu.org/news/

Fig. 10.6 Stucture of IAMU

Exercise

Chapter.10

1. Write down key words in this chapter.

2. Summarize the content in this chapter.

✓ **Speed Quiz** – Explain the meaning of the word and Answer the word

✍ Practice

1. Image the word

2. Make the sentence

3. Make your team and story

4. Set the role

5. Presentation with video recording

6. Self-evaluation

7. Feedback

Presentation Evaluation sheet

Team Presenter

Title

1. Topic clear

1	2	3	4	5	6	7	8	9	10

2. Voice clearance

1	2	3	4	5	6	7	8	9	10

3. Presentation Material

1	2	3	4	5	6	7	8	9	10

4. Maritime Word

1	2	3	4	5	6	7	8	9	10

5. Grammar

1	2	3	4	5	6	7	8	9	10

6. Expression (Body language)

1	2	3	4	5	6	7	8	9	10

7. pace

1	2	3	4	5	6	7	8	9	10

8. story structure

1	2	3	4	5	6	7	8	9	10

9. Q & A

1	2	3	4	5	6	7	8	9	10

10. Overall score

1	2	3	4	5	6	7	8	9	10

✓ **Feedback opinion**

Date ____________

Evaluator ____________

11

Stakeholders in Shipping Industry

Fig. 11.1 Stakeholders in shipping industry

11.1 Private Sector

11.1.1 Ship owner

The company that owns the asset ship. Shipowners invest their money, with or without the financial assistance from banks or private funds, in new buildings or purchasing second-hand ships.

11.1.2 Charters

(1) Time charter

Time charters, whether for a period or for a trip, are those under which, in return for the payment of hire, the vessel's employment is put under the orders of the charterers, while possession remains with the owners who provide the crew and pay the ordinary running costs, characteristically excluding specific voyage costs such as fuel and cargo handling and port charges, which are paid for by the charterers.

(2) Voyage charter

Voyage charters are those by which the owner agrees to perform one or more designated voyages in return for the payment of freight and (when appropriate) demurrage; the costs of, and responsibility for, cargo handling are left to the terms of the specific agreement.

(3) Demise (bareboat) charter

Demise charters are those by which, in return for payment of hire, possession of the chartered ship is given to the charterers, who provide crew and all supplies, pay all running costs and undertake the responsibility of shipowner to those whose goods are carried on the vessel.

(4) Slot charter

Slot charters involve the chartering of a guaranteed number of container spaces either on a period or a voyage basis.

11.1.3 Ship management company

A ship management company is the company that is mainly responsible for the crewing, technical maintenance and supply of food and spare parts. Ships are expensive, depreciating assets that require high quality maintenance. Proper maintenance is often crucial for achieving higher freight rates by ensuring the high quality and safe transportation of goods they carry. Proper maintenance of ships is largely dictated by specialised engineering companies, known as Classification Societies or simply Classes

11.1.4 Freight forwarder

A freight forwarder, forwarder, or forwarding agent, is a person or company that organizes shipments for individuals or corporations to get goods from the manufacturer or producer to a market, customer or final point of distribution

11.1.5 S&P Broker

A Sale & Purchase (S&P) Broker is the intermediary role that facilitates the process of buying and selling of ships. Like Chartering brokers, the S&P brokers maintain wide networks of ship owners and banks so as to identify good matches and opportunities for selling and buying a ship.

11.1.6 Cargo owner

The owner of any goods and any bailor, bailee consignor shipper consignee or other respective agents in relation thereto

11.1.7 Marine insurer

Marine Insurance is a type of insurance designed to provide coverage for the transportation of goods either on the ocean or by land as well as damage to the waterborne instrument of conveyance and to the liability for third parties arising out of the process.

11.2 Public Sector

11.2.1 Maritime administration

Maritime administrations or flag state administrations are the executive bodies of each government responsible for carrying out the shipping responsibilities of the state, and are tasked to administer national shipping and boating issues and laws within their territorial waters and for vessels flagged in that country or that fall under their jurisdiction.

The main functions are:

- Government policy for ships and boating, marine safety in general, seaworthiness, safe construction and stability
- Policing Dangerous goods being carried, Navigation safety, Safe manning, Certificates of Competency/ licenses for crew
- Health, safety and welfare of crew, civil search and rescue
- Prevention and combating marine pollution and response, investigation of marine accidents
- Represents country on IMO and other International Conventions

(1) Ministry of oceans and fisherie, Republic of Korea

MOF has an executive responsibility for marine - related work encompassing shipping & port industry, fisheries industry, fishing community & coastal city, marine environment, maritime safety, marine tourism & leisure activity and maritime territory.

(2) United States maritime administration

The United States Maritime Administration (MARAD) is an agency of the United States Department of Transportation. MARAD supports the technical aspects of America's maritime transportation infrastructure - things like ships and shipping, port and vessel operations, national security, environment, and safety.

(3) Ministry of transport of the People's Republic of China

The Ministry of Transport (MOT) of the People's Republic of China is an executive agency under the State Council responsible for road, water and air transportation.

(4) Ministry of land, infrastructure, transport and tourism, Japan

The Ministry of Land, Infrastructure, Transport and Tourism is a ministry of the Japanese government. It is responsible for one-third of all the laws and orders in Japan, and is the largest Japanese ministry in terms of employees, as well as the second-largest executive agency of the Japanese government after the Ministry of Defense. The ministry oversees four external agencies including the Japan Coast Guard and the Japan Tourism Agency.

(5) Maritime and coastguard agency, United Kingdom

The Maritime and Coastguard Agency (MCA) is an executive agency of the United Kingdom working to prevent the loss of lives at sea and is responsible, through the Secretary of State for Transport to Parliament, for implementing British and international maritime law and safety policy.

(6) Australian maritime safety authority

Australian Maritime Safety Authority (AMSA) is an Australian statutory authority responsible for the regulation and safety oversight of Australia's shipping fleet and management of Australia's international maritime obligations.

11.2.2 Coast guard

Coast guard is a maritime security organization of a particular country. The term embraces wide range of responsibilities in different countries, from being a heavily armed military force with customs and security duties to being a volunteer organization tasked with search and rescue without law enforcement authority. In most countries, a typical coast guard's functions are distinct from those of the navy (a military service) and the transit police (a law enforcement agency), while in certain countries has similarities to both.

Fig. 11.2 Korea coast guard

Exercise

Chapter.11

1. Write down key words in this chapter.

2. Summarize the content in this chapter.

✓ **Speed Quiz** – Explain the meaning of the word and Answer the word

Practice

1. Image the word

2. Make the sentence

3. Make your team and story

4. Set the role

5. Presentation with video recording

6. Self-evaluation

7. Feedback

Presentation Evaluation sheet

Team Presenter

Title

1. Topic clear

1	2	3	4	5	6	7	8	9	10

2. Voice clearance

1	2	3	4	5	6	7	8	9	10

3. Presentation Material

1	2	3	4	5	6	7	8	9	10

4. Maritime Word

1	2	3	4	5	6	7	8	9	10

5. Grammar

1	2	3	4	5	6	7	8	9	10

6. Expression (Body language)

1	2	3	4	5	6	7	8	9	10

7. pace

1	2	3	4	5	6	7	8	9	10

8. story structure

1	2	3	4	5	6	7	8	9	10

9. Q & A

1	2	3	4	5	6	7	8	9	10

10. Overall score

1	2	3	4	5	6	7	8	9	10

✓ **Feedback opinion**

Date ______________ Evaluator ______________

Appendix

1. Autonomous Shipping

https://www.imo.org/en/MediaCentre/HotTopics/Pages/Autonomous-shipping.aspx

2. Initial IMO GHG Strategy

https://www.imo.org/en/MediaCentre/HotTopics/Pages/Reducing-greenhouse-gas-emissions-from-ships.aspx

3. Ammonia as a Marine Fuel

https://www.dnv.com/Publications/ammonia-as-a-marine-fuel-191385

4. Draft Interim Guidelines for Ships Using Fuel Cells Agreed by Sub - Committee

https://www.imo.org/en/MediaCentre/Pages/WhatsNew-1636.aspx

5. Greenflation Hits Shipping

https://gcaptain.com/greenflation-shipping/

6. Blockchain and Shipping: Can it Work?

https://www.hellenicshippingnews.com/blockchain-and-shipping-can-it-work/

7. Seafarers Desperately Need Prompt Access to Medical Care Say ILO and International Maritime Organization

https://www.ilo.org/global/about-the-ilo/newsroom/news/WCMS_822132/lang—en/index.htm

8. Daewoo Shipbuilding & Marine Engineering v Songa Offshore Equinox Ltd [2020] EWHC 2353 (TCC)

https://iistl.blog/2020/10/09/preliminary-issue-on-a-question-of-construction-what-happens-next/

9. Cyber risk: The emerging cyber threat to industrial control systems

https://www.lloyds.com/news-and-insights/risk-reports/library/icsreport

10. The European shipping industry in a nutshell - ECSA

https://www.ecsa.eu/sites/default/files/publications/ECSA_brochure_0.pdf

11. Industry firsts: World's 1st eco-friendly ships in 2021

https://www.offshore-energy.biz/industry-firsts-worlds-1st-eco-friendly-ships-in-2021/

12. How can shipping be more environmentally friendly?

https://www.rmg.co.uk/stories/topics/how-can-shipping-be-more-environmentally-friendly

13. Coronavirus disease (COVID-19) Pandemic

https://www.imo.org/en/MediaCentre/HotTopics/Pages/Coronavirus.aspx

14. IMO 2020 – cutting sulphur oxide emissions

https://www.imo.org/en/MediaCentre/HotTopics/Pages/Sulphur-2020.aspx

15. Shipping in polar waters

https://www.imo.org/en/MediaCentre/HotTopics/Pages/polar-default.aspx

16. Hydrogen Forecast to 2050

https://www.dnv.com/focus-areas/hydrogen/forecast-to-2050.html

17. Power-to-X: The key to decarbonization

https://www.man-es.com/energy-storage/solutions/power-to-x

18. Shipboard organization

https://knowledgeofsea.com/shipboard-organisation/

19. The different types of propulsion on ships

https://shipinsight.com/guide/the-different-types-of-propulsion-on-ships

20. A list of inspections and surveys deck officers on ships should be aware of

https://www.marineinsight.com/maritime-law/a-list-of-inspections-and-surveys-deck-officers-on-ships-should-be-aware-of/

21. Accident investigation publications – European Maritime Safety Agency

https://www.emsa.europa.eu/accident-investigation-publications/annual-overview.html

Maritime Word

▼I

▼K

▼L

▼M

Prof. Dr. HyunWook Doo

2007 - Present. Professor, Korea Institute of Maritime and Fisheries Technology
2001 - 2007. Surveyor, Korea Maritime Transportation Safety Authority
1997 - 2000. Marine Engineer, Hyundai Merchant Marine Co., Ltd
2012. Korea Maritime & Ocean University, Ph.D. in Law

Prof. Dr. DaeWon Kim

2020 - Present. Professor, Korea Maritime & Ocean University
2018 - 2020. Researcher, Institute of Automation in University of Rostock(Germany)
2013 - 2015. Researcher, ISSIMS Institute in University of Wismar(Germany)
2008 - 2011. Teaching Associate, Korea Maritime & Ocean University
2005 - 2008. Navigational Officer, Keoyang Shipping and Hanjin Shipping
2019. University of Rostock(Germany), Ph.D. in Engineering in Maritime systems

Prof. Dr. SeongWan Kim

2020 - Present. Professor, Korea Institute of Maritime Fisheries Technology
2011 - 2020. Head of PrimeServ Academy Busan, MAN Energy Soultions
2006 - 2011. Marine Engineer, Hyundai Merchant Marine Co., Ltd
2021. Korea Maritime & Ocean University, Ph.D. in Marine Engineering System

Prof. Dr. SangSeop Lim

2020 - Present. Professor, Korea Maritime & Ocean University
2020. Professor, PaiChai University
2018 - 2020. Lecturer, Korea Maritime & Ocean University
2007 - 2012. Navigational Officer, Hyundai Merchant Marine Co., Ltd
2018. Korea Maritime & Ocean University, Ph.D in Shipping Management

Prof. Dr. HyeonMin Jeon

2021 - Present. Professor, Korea Maritime & Ocean University
2020 - 2021. Researcher, Korea Maritime & Ocean University
2010 - 2015. Marine Engineer, STX Panocean Co., Ltd
2020. Korea Maritime & Ocean University, Ph.D. in Marine Engineering System

Prof. Dr. JungHwan Choi

2021 Present. Foreign Expert, Law School, Dalian Maritime University (China)
2020 - 2021. Lecturer, Korea Maritime & Ocean University
2017 - 2020. Research Fellow Specializing on the EU Maritime Industry, Maritime Cluster Networking in Korea
2013 - 2016. Teaching Associate, Korea Maritime & Ocean University
2008 - 2013. Marine Engineer, Hanjin Shipping Co., Ltd
2020. University of Exeter (UK), Law School, Ph.D. in Maritime Law